Serials Automation

for Acquisition and Inventory Control

Edited by
William Gray Potter and Arlene Farber Sirkin

Papers from the Institute
Milwaukee, September 4–5, 1980
Library and Information Technology Association
American Library Association

American Library Association
Chicago 1981

Text designed by Vladimir Reichl

Cover designed by Ellen Pettengell

Composed by Steno Bureau, Urbana, Illinois,
in Baskerville on IBM Magnetic Tape Composer

Printed on 50# Antique Glatfelter, a pH-
neutral stock, and bound in 10-point
Carolina cover stock, by Imperial
Printing Company

Library of Congress Cataloging in Publication Data
Main entry under title:

Serials automation for acquisition and inventory control.

Proceedings of a conference held Sept. 4-5, 1980 in
Milwaukee and sponsored by the Library and Information
Technology Association.
Bibliography: p.
1. Serials control systems — Automation — Congresses.
2. Acquisitions (Libraries) — Automation — Congresses.
I. Potter, William Gray. II. Sirkin, Arlene Farber.
III. Library and Information Technology Association
(U.S.)
Z692.S5S476   025.3′432′02854   81-10798
ISBN 0-8389-3267-3 (pbk.)   AACR2

Contents

Contents

Acknowledgments

This publication is a result of the Serials Automation: Acquisition and Inventory Control Institute. We owe a great deal of thanks to the many people who made that institute possible. Kaye Gapen and the entire LITA Program Planning Committee provided constructive criticism and many suggestions. Don Hammer, LITA program director, and his staff ably handled the many details and minutiae that allowed the institute to flow smoothly. Finally, we would like to express our gratitude to all the speakers and participants whose presentations and questions made this publication possible.

Arlene Farber Sirkin
U.S. Army Audiovisual Center
Washington, D.C.

Introduction

The Library and Information Technology Association (LITA) of the American Library Association sponsored the institute entitled "Serials Automation: Acquisition and Inventory Control" held in Milwaukee on September 4-5, 1980. The last LITA institute, and indeed the last national conference, on serials automation was held in 1975 when the division was still known as the Information Science and Automation Division.[1] In the years since that institute, many developments combined to produce new situations which commanded national interest and made a second LITA institute on automated serials control desirable:

OCLC's check-in system was introduced.

PHILSOM, already successful in 1975, expanded and went online.

Major subscription agencies began to offer new automated control functions to clients, with online check-in on the horizon.

Northwestern University, the National Library of Medicine, the University of California at Los Angeles, and other institutions extended the capabilities of existing systems.

The Research Library Information Network (RLIN), the Washington Library Network (WLN), and others began to consider serials control subsystems.

Glyn Evans, in his introduction to the LARC proceedings of 1973, defined three modes of automated serials control: acquisition control, bibliographic control, and inventory control.[2] Because no single conference could adequately cover all three of these modes and because the earlier LITA institute was principally concerned with the issues of bibliographic control in automated serials systems, the topic of the latest LITA institute was limited to acquisition and inventory control.

The institute examined the role of automation in these functions. It provided theoretical and practical discussion of the issues involved and attempted to impart to those in attendance a firm understanding of the past, present, and future states of automated serials control. Over 275 registrants from throughout the United States and Canada attended the institute, and judging from the written evaluations collected afterwards, it was very well received. The papers in this volume are based upon selected presentations from the institute.

Dan Tonkery delivered the keynote presentation and his paper offers an overview of the historical and philosophical context of automated serials control. The check-in function, the central operation in any automated serials control system, is examined in detail by Jim Fayollat. The relationship between the check-in record and the holdings record and the often neglected correspondence between detailed holdings and circulation are discussed by Susan Miller as part of a paper on inventory control. The expanding capabilities of vendors in the area of serials control, including the potential of off-site check-in by agents, are analyzed by Betsy Humphreys. At the institute a panel of vendor representatives discussed systems for automated serial control that were available or about to be introduced. An edited transcription of that panel discussion is included in these published proceedings. As a library becomes more dependent upon an automated serials control system, patron access to that system becomes more important. This is the topic of Velma Veniziano's paper. Michael Gorman, the final speaker at the institute, has prepared a paper on the role of automated serials control in the future organization of the library.

Demonstrations of systems by vendors and by libraries or networks with notable systems were a major feature of the institute. The number of presentations was kept small in order to allow time for those in attendance to examine these systems. Because these demonstrations were important to the success of the institute, it was essential to include some description of them in the published proceedings. Four of the systems are described in the transcription of the panel discussion. Five others are described in an appendix.

Each of the registrants received a bibliography prepared by Gary Pitkin of items concerning serials automation published since

1974. For the published proceedings, Mr. Pitkin has prepared annotations for those items which were most relevant to the theme of the institute.

William Gray Potter
University of Illinois
Urbana-Champaign

REFERENCES

1. The earlier institute was held in Atlanta in October 1974 and in San Francisco in November 1975. The Atlanta meeting is summarized in Mary Kay Daniels, "Automated Serials Control: National and International Considerations," *Journal of Library Automation* 8 (June 1975; no. 2); 127-46.

2. Glyn Evans, "State of the Art" in William H. Axford, ed., *Proceedings of the LARC Institute on Automated Serials Systems* (Tempe, Arizona: LARC Association, 1973).

Evolution of Automated Serials Control: Technical, Philosophical, and Political Issues

DAN TONKERY

My first action after agreeing to prepare this paper was to attempt to locate published proceedings of the 1973 LARC (Association for Library Automation Research Communications) serials meeting in my local university library.[1] After trying to determine the cataloging treatment, I proceeded to the card catalog only to find no entry for the published proceedings. Not wishing to give up, I then went to the serials department, thinking that perhaps this was one of those unanalyzed serials titles buried in our 50,000 Kardex records.

Interpreting the Kardex information proved to be an even greater challenge than the card catalog because there is only one access point and that bibliographic entry is selected by the serials department. After locating five or six titles that could possibly be what I was looking for, I proceeded to the stacks.

Finding other LARC materials, but not the desired item, I contacted the library school and, to make a long story short, they could not locate the proceedings either. (Their entries were even more difficult than the serials department's.)

My final attempt proved successful. I searched OCLC, using the state holdings screen display and found that a nearby state university library had a copy, which I then obtained on interlibrary loan.

That was my first action. My second action was even more interesting. I began a literature search using several of the commercial online databases and retrieved 30-40 promising articles.

Dan Tonkery is associate university librarian for technical and bibliographical product services at the University of California-Los Angeles Library.

Most of the titles were serials as you might expect, and I determined that they were owned by UCLA. That was the easy part. The difficult part came in going to the stacks and trying to determine their status: whether the titles were at the bindery, missing, or checked out. I was fortunate in that in addition to the printed sources of material my search also retrieved several ERIC documents which were held in microfiche. I obtained the microfiche and began reading 300-400 pages of research reports. I now understand the user's complaints about microforms.

After spending several weeks subjected to manual serials records, I had to disregard my first hypothesis that the primary reason that serials automation had not proceeded was simply that it was not needed and that the manual system was more effective. In fact, nothing could be further from the truth.

I would like to offer a brief historical perspective and present a philosophical discussion of automated serials control. Although the most significant advances in library recordkeeping have occurred in the past fifty years with the introduction of computer technology, the history of recordkeeping reflects a search for more efficient ways of gathering, recording, and handling data to keep pace with the increasing volume of data produced by various elements of society.

A short history of data-recording techniques demonstrates that our basic need to count has influenced the development of techniques and technology. From requirements in commercial accounting in the early thirteenth century, we have the developments which led to our modern computer technology. Between the thirteenth and nineteenth centuries significant improvements, such as Pascal's calculator in 1692 and Babbage's analytical engines in 1834, influenced the development of modern-day calculators, and the first-generation computers produced in 1946.[2]

In early libraries, data-recording techniques were used in the processing of materials. As new inventions became available for general use, the library incorporated the data-recording devices without any major problem. Three such inventions were welcome additions to the library. The first, which appeared in the mid-1680s, has been almost universally accepted as a data-recording device. Even today, the graphite rod enclosed in wood, better known as the pencil, is still a major device used in library processing. The second invention in 1820 was the first major breakthrough to assist the library in maintaining permanent records. The production of pens with slip-in points enabled the library to provide access to the collection through recording bibliographic information in a book catalog. An excellent example of a product created by this invention is the book catalog at the Bodleian Library at Oxford University.

The third invention was accepted only reluctantly, since many librarians favored the hand-created book catalog. The manual typewriter, patented in 1868, has become the working tool of almost every technical services staff member. For over one hundred years, this data-recording device has been the mainstay of record creation and information transfer. Although the electric typewriter has been available since the early twenties, most technical services departments are still required to use the manual devices from the past.

Since libraries had taken advantage of the data-recording devices of the past, one would expect the continuation of this trend with the mechanical system of recording, computing, and tabulating developed by Dr. Hollerith in 1890 for the Census Bureau. While punch-card technology for data processing was available in 1900, it was not until the 1930s that a number of significant technical advances took place which further expanded the use of punch-card equipment for library processing. Of these advances, the ability of cards to hold more information and the availability of machines to handle alphabetic information increased the scope of jobs for which the equipment could be used in a library environment. Given these two advances and the increase in speed and versatility of these machines, the library profession began to consider punch-card applications.

The earliest recorded use of the punch-card technology in a library setting was reported in 1936 in *Library Journal* by Ralph Parker, the loan librarian at the University of Texas, Austin. This application used punched cards to support circulation work, and Parker reported "that a wide field of library development is about to be opened. College and university libraries especially can make their records more flexible and yet more simple by use of machines."[3] After this early work by the University of Texas in circulation, the library staff continued to develop applications. Moffit, also from Texas, reported in the January 1946 *College and Research Libraries* his success with using a punched-card record system in serials acquisitions.[4]

From the early 1930s until the 1960s, punch-card data processing or unit-record equipment was the major method of data processing for library automation support, and serials automation in particular. Libraries continued to use the unit-record equipment. The limitations of first-generation computer equipment — limited main memory, expensive secondary storage, system reliability, high operating costs, and the high cost of developing machine-language software systems — prevented any serious consideration of first-generation computer technology by the library community.

In the early 1960s, even with the improvements in second-generation equipment, many libraries found it more economical to use the punch-card systems and relied on the computer only for printing support. These systems included the support of preparing serials holdings lists, handling subscriptions, checking in issues, producing claims, preparing bindery lists, and controlling routing. However, the punch-card system by its very nature limited the size of the serials operation which could feasibly be controlled. With the punched-card system, any collection over 1,500 titles required a high volume of card handling which soon became a drain on the system.[5]

Toward the end of the second-generation computer systems (1959-64), a number of libraries began projects which can be considered pioneering efforts in the field of serials automation. These were the first systems that were not straight listing applications, but contained software developed to perform specific functions on the data. Even though these systems still used punch cards for input, the computer manipulated the data and produced products which required complicated sorting. Most of these early systems were developed in the fields of medicine, science, and technology. Of particular interest were the applications at the University of California, San Diego, Washington University School of Medicine, Purdue University, and the University of California, Los Angeles.[6] Each of these early serials systems applications has been documented in the literature so I will offer only some general comments.

The early check-in systems had many similarities, such as the maintenance of the file on magnetic tape, the use of punched cards as the input mechanism, the production of various lists, and operation in a batch mode. Each system involved the use of an arrival card that was computer produced in advance for each issue predicted to arrive in a given month. When the corresponding title and issue were received, the punched card was pulled and a batch program updated all of the recent receipts. Any cards remaining after a fixed period of time were for periodical issues which had

4

not arrived. These cards were then collected and used for claiming.

Several variations of the arrival-card system were used. Some produced the next month's expected issues, some produced cards for the next issue after receiving the latest issue on a one-for-one basis, and some produced a quarterly punched card. Each had problems involving the limitation of punched cards, such as the 80-column limit which often prevented the use of the full serial title.

Even with limitations, these early systems enabled the libraries to provide improved access to their serial collection. This level of automation utilized the unit-record equipment and stored programs, but did not significantly reduce the staff levels required to support serials processing. In fact many libraries retained their manual files.[7]

Apart from technological achievements, other factors combined to provide a strong impetus for serials automation development. In 1957, with the successful launching of the Russian satellite, the federal government began a national campaign to support the scientific and technical community. Before 1940, the direct investment in research and development (R & D) was modest. By 1962, federal expenditures in R & D had grown to nearly 12 billion dollars and accounted for two-thirds of all R & D funds in the United States. By 1969, the amount had risen to 27 billion dollars. This tremendous growth in resources had not only a major impact on the complexion and motivation of scientific and technological pursuits, but also had a crucial impact on the phenomenal growth of information disseminated as a direct result of this increase in spending.[8]

With this growth in information came the legitimate concern by the scientific community that some methods for improved access were necessary. As early as 1958, the Science Advisory Committee, chaired by William Baker, brought this problem to the attention of the President.[9] This concern was widely recognized by three additional presidential committees. These committees were convinced that adequate communication was a prerequisite for strong science and technology and that the technical communications system had to be a concern of government. The Weinberg Report, in describing the information problem, stated "Science and technology can flourish only if each scientist interacts with his colleagues and his predecessors. . . . The ideas and data that are the substance of science and technology are embodied in the literature . . . ."[10]

During the 1960s the federal government supported an ever increasing amount of R & D which led to what has been called the "information crisis." Libraries began to feel the pressure of this national effort. There was a sudden increase in the number of journals published and a corresponding demand for access to this information.

Without any single solution to the problem, but feeling some responsibility, the federal government did begin to support libraries in various ways including specific funding in the Higher Education Act of 1965 and the Medical Library Association Act of 1965. In addition, other funding agencies began to be concerned about the problem of access to information. With the federal government concern, as well as private funding agencies, the library community began to see the sponsorship of several automation projects, including some involving serials automation.

Even with the assistance of outside funding and the availability of third-generation computer equipment which, by 1965, offered cost effective online service, increased storage capacity, advanced operating systems, and time-sharing capability, most serials automation projects failed. Those who attempted circulation systems succeeded.

Both circulation and serials check-in functions seemed well suited to computer processing. They are both high volume, repetitive operations with complex recordkeeping requirements. Those who tackled the problems of circulation control were for the most part successful, at least for routine tasks. However, even today, few turnkey systems will handle the complex circulation requirements of the large research library. Serials control and especially serials check-in proved to be a far more complex programming problem than designers had originally projected.[11]

Serials automation has not made significant gains beyond elementary listing operations despite the fact that from a technological standpoint the computer hardware and software have been available and economically feasible since the early seventies. It is difficult to identify any major technical obstacle to the successful automation of serials, at least at the local level. Perhaps the failures in the sixties gave serials automation, and especially check-in systems, some well-deserved bad press which convinced library administrators not to commit library resources to serials automation projects. Another theory, which has not been proven nor discussed in the literature, has to do with the workload in serials departments. With the tremendous increase in the volume of publications received, most, if not all, serials departments have not received sufficient additional staffing to handle the workload. There is a constant effort just to maintain the check-in operation, with few departments having the necessary staff to do claiming and perform the other related serials processing tasks. Working under near hardship conditions, serials department managers have not been able to perform the analysis required to develop suitable specifications for serials automation. In past automation attempts, computer specialists, including system analysts, were brought into departments and attempted to develop systems without an appreciation of the problems inherent in serials processing. Given the complexity of serials, it is little wonder that many projects ended in failure and frustration.

Because of severe understaffing in serials departments and the lack of detailed specifications for serials automation at the local level, the library community was satisfied to wait for a national approach to serials automation or to wait for a bibliographic utility or other vendor to offer the service. However, this outside alternative was not universally considered to be the most practical since the record management problems related to serials ordering and accounting, cataloging, receiving, claiming, and binding are all interrelated and, many believe, should be handled as a total system at the local level.

At the national level, the problems with serials check-in and serials automation were further compounded by the lack of agreement over serials bibliographic control in both national and international arenas. At the International Service Automation Division Institute in 1975, Mary Sauer and others reviewed the status of serials bibliographic control. Out of that discussion came a clear picture that bibliographic control of serials is an uncompleted evolutionary process. *AACR,* International Standard Bibliographic Description for Serials, and International Serials Data System (ISDS) all have different definitions as to what comprises the title of a serial and what constitutes a title change.[12] To add to this confusion, there is no universal acceptance as to the definition of a serial. Even at an individual institution, the same title may receive different treatment. Few acquisitions departments would agree with serials departments over what is a serial. Cataloging departments would further disagree on the interpretation of the standard definition. For the purpose of this discussion, a serial is any title received and processed by the serials department. A full definition may be found in the glossary of the *AACR2* cataloging rules.

7

A significant part of the problem of serials bibliographic control exists because of the nature of serials in general. Because of their indefinite continuance and their ability to change names, reproduce, die, yet be reborn, divide into two or three separate publications and remain dormant or inactive for years, the general library community has developed a type of phobia in dealing with serials control problems.

There are specific problems in dealing with serials bibliographic control, especially in cataloging, which have an impact on the development of a serials database which can be accepted nationally. Each problem is further compounded by the size and age of the individual library. While attempts have been made to solve the issues relating to choice of entry, form of entry, and bibliographic description, the library community still remains divided over the acceptance of international standards. To further compound the situation, the move from the ALA code with its latest entry rules to the successive entry rules of the *AACR* code have been extremely painful for large research libraries with their complex local bibliographic files.

While the international standards are not prescriptive in terms of authorship responsibility, one cannot overlook the influence the *Guidelines for ISDS* has had on reinforcing the concept of title entry for the choice of main entry. The influence of international standards and serials cataloging in particular has been the subject of several articles. Paul Fasana offers a good description of the problem in the March 1976 issue of the *Journal of Library Automation*. In that article, he expresses a serious concern for the impact that international standards are having on library cataloging practices, especially when radical and substantive changes have been made in *AACR2* to meet these standards.[13]

In addition to recognizable serials bibliographic standards, the lack of a national serials database severely limited the progress in serials automation at the national level. Two noteworthy attempts at developing a national serials database have been the National Serials Data Program (NSDP) and CONSER (CONversion of SERials). Both of these programs have been discussed in library literature so I will only use them to illustrate that the library community has recognized the urgent need to develop an authoritative serials bibliographic database to support serials automation. This authoritative database would be used to support serials automation projects on a national, regional, or local level. The continued development of local union lists as an aid to accessing information was recognized as unmanageable and certainly not cost effective. The problems at the local level with bibliographic record incompatibility, data conversion, redundancy, and limited bibliographic structure were considered serious by most library managers. An authoritative national serials database is a highly desirable goal and long overdue.

Without a machine-readable bibliographic record of some type, it is difficult to build a serials automation project. While at the local level it might be argued that a full MARC record is not required, the lack of standardized bibliographic data is a major problem in transferring or sharing that information with other libraries. A report by Radke and Berger discusses the technical difficulties in merging different bibliographic records for the same title from the libraries of the University of California.[14] It is very difficult as well as expensive to undertake a union listing project with nonstandardized data. This problem is further compounded by the lack of an authority control structure or mechanism. Most of us are aware of the problems in searching bibliographic databases only to find multiple records for the same serial title.

The development of a national serials database based on authoritative bibliographic records and the resolution of controversial issues in serials cataloging will stimulate serials automation projects at the national level. The widespread availability of the CONSER database from OCLC, Inc., has made a tremendous improvement in the access to critical bibliographic information. At today's prices, the cost of local conversion of serials records into machine-readable form would prevent most libraries from even considering serials automation projects. From my own experience with our conversion effort at UCLA, which is funded by a Title II-C grant, the data conversion costs are over thirteen dollars per record for direct costs only. At this price, libraries would not be able to convert their serials records without outside support. The CONSER file is a national resource which will pay dividends for years to come. Each CONSER member is contributing to the building of a national serials database. The cost of participating is an institutional responsibility which can be an added burden, but the benefit is worth the effort.

Another problem with successful serials automation projects has been the lack of a standardized holdings statement. Without this holdings statement standard, it has been difficult to share information, merge holdings records, or produce serials products without a substantial amount of manual editing. The lack of standardized holdings statements has long been a recognized problem. While *AACR* rule 163 refers to holdings statements, it only gives general information about holdings and does not give any guidance on such questions as double or triple numbering systems, mixed-media holdings, or specific notation for missing issues. In the absence of standards, most libraries have based their holdings statements on the pattern established by the *Union List of Serials* and *New Serial Titles*.[15]

After a proliferation of union lists and other serials listing projects, the problem of serials holdings statements at the summary level has been investigated, and an ANSI (American National Standards Institute) subcommittee chaired by Glyn Evans finally released an ANSI standard for summary serials holdings in 1979.[16] This standard went through eight drafts before being accepted by the voting members. In the end a number of compromises were made which will not please some. However, we now have a standard which can be followed and implemented.

In addition to the summary serials holdings statements, we still need a detailed holdings statement. Another ANSI subcommittee is working on this problem. The future looks promising for national standards at both the summary level and the detailed level. Both of these standards will enhance serials automation efforts.

On the national level, we spent the seventies in building a national serials database, developing national standards for holdings information, resolving many of the bibliographic problems relating to choice and form of entry, and adopting international standards for the transcription and display of bibliographic information (ISBD-S).

While we have considered these general intellectual issues in the bibliographic control of serials, computer technology has continued to make rapid advances in both the hardware and software areas. This computer evolution is increasing tenfold every decade. Libraries can take advantage of the continued price/performance improvements available now for serials automation. With the recent technological trends, libraries of all types should consider the exploitation of online technology for not only bibliographic searching but for database building, for file maintenance, and for the routine repetitive tasks associated with the technical processing of library materials, especially serials processing.

We must develop local systems that use the bibliographic information from a national serials database. With the volume of activity and the interrelationship of serials processing functions, it will continue to be difficult to perform serials processing functions at a remote site until telecommunication service is responsive and cost effective. While some large libraries may depend on a large computer system at the campus or share a system with another organization, most libraries will select some form of large minicomputer linked to a bibliographic utility or other large regional or state computer center as the most desirable computer configuration. The utility would supply the initial bibliographic records, the local library adding their local processing information to the local computer system.

From a functional point of view, this local processing includes online ordering, receiving, claiming, binding, and accounting. With a printer available, the library could review all output reports, such as serials lists, bindery notices, claim forms, and other products. Since serials processing functions are interrelated, having only one or two functions supported by a utility is not the most desirable option. The only way of improving the efficiency of serials processing is to have all serials processing functions under the control of the same computer system.

Even though minicomputer hardware has the capacity to handle the large files of serials, we still have the problem of software development and maintenance. Since each individual library may not be able to absorb the cost of systems development, this development effort should be undertaken on a regional basis with an organized network or perhaps a bibliographic utility. With research and development staff working on the serials automation project, the software could be developed in a short time. However, this is a matter of priority, not necessarily technical difficulty. One must decide whether circulation systems, acquisitions systems, or other systems take priority over serials systems. To date, serials systems have taken a back seat to circulation systems and others because of priorities set by library managers.

If we are unable to obtain the research and development support required to link minicomputers with the utilities or to use the national database, we are not without at least one other choice.

During the past two years the serials subscription agents have begun to show an interest in the problems of serials control. Much of their serials automation expertise comes out of automating their subscription control and accounting operations. With additional software development, they will be able to support receiving, claiming, and binding as well as to provide management reports to individual clients. These systems may offer an attractive alternative for serials automation support in many libraries. Subscription agents such as Faxon and Ebsco have begun to recognize the problem of serials control and have committed resources for research and development of serials automation systems.

During the 1980s, libraries will continue to take advantage of new technology, and online serials control will become more commonplace. Bibliographic utilities and regional networks will become more active in serials automation support. Subscription agents will begin to play a larger role in the control of serials.

Online serials control is not impossible. Several libraries in the early 1970s, including Northwestern University and the University of California, Los Angeles, demonstrated that online real-time integrated serials automation systems that control check-in, claiming, binding, accounting, ordering, and a host of output products can be designed and implemented and be cost effective.[17] Online real-time systems such as OCLC do support partial serials processing functions, but are not complete serials systems. In addition, many of the early batch systems are now using online input techniques, but still depend heavily on batch operations for record maintenance. In the medical community, the National Library of Medicine's SERLINE and the Washington University School of Medicine's PHILSOM system are supported with online technology for part of the serials operation.

Serials automation projects are not handicapped by technological problems, by bibliographic unknowns, or by lack of talent for software development. The basic problem is one of priority and competition for limited resources. It is difficult for a library manager to support serials automation when faced with declining budgets, faculty and student pressure to keep the stacks in order, increasing volumes of circulation, deteriorating collections, cataloging backlogs, card catalog filing backlogs, and inadequate physical space to house existing collections. The concern for the problem in serials automation is diminished by the myriad problems that a library manager must face each day.

Library managers must recognize that the successful automation of serials control offers immediate benefit to the public service offered by any library. The availability of current check-in information, the successful management of serials budgets, the improved service potential from a current claiming and binding system, and the availability of management information all serve as stimuli to proceed with serials automation projects.

The library of the future will rely heavily on the advantages of computerization. Most technical processing operations will be controlled or supported by some form of automation. We need to take advantage of the existing technological achievements of the national serials database now under development and assign a high priority to the automation of serials processing activities. As labor costs continue to escalate, the cost performance ratio for the computer continue to improve. Shifting much of our repetitive, time-consuming, intensive clerical work in serials control to the computer can increase productivity and enable existing staff to improve their service capability. Automation can have a positive effect on the operation of a serials department. Library management must assign a high priority to the development of successful automation projects in the area of serials control.

REFERENCES

1. William H. Axford, *Proceedings of the LARC Institute on Automated Serials Systems* (Tempe, Arizona: LARC Association, 1973).

2. Jeffrey Frates and William Moldrup. *Introduction to the Computer: An Integrative Approach* (Englewood Cliffs, N.J.: Prentice-Hall, 1980).

3. Ralph H. Parker, "The Punched Card Method in Circulation Work," *Library Journal* 61 (Dec. 1936): 903-5.

4. A. Moffitt, "Punched Card Records in Serials Automation," *College and Research Libraries* 7 (Jan. 1946): 10-13.

5. I.A. Worheit, *Library Automation — Computerized Serials Control* (New York: IBM Corporation, 1971).

6. Fred W. Roper, "A Computer-Based Serials Control System for a Large Biomedical Library," *American Documentation* 19 (1968 no. 2): 151-57; J. Fayollat and D. Luck, "Computer-Based Serials Control System, Biomedical Library, UCLA," *American Documentation* 20 (1969 no. 4): 385; George Vdovin, "The Serials Computer Project, University of California Library, San Diego," in Wesley C. Simonton, ed., *Information Retrieval Today: Papers Presented at the Institute Conducted by the Library School and the Center for Continuation Study, University of Minnesota, September 19-22, 1962.* (Minneapolis: Center for Continuation Study, University of Minnesota, 1962), pp. 109-18; Irwin H. Pizer et al., "Mechanization of Library Procedures in the Medium-Sized Medical Library: I. The Serial Record," *Bulletin of the Medical Library Association* 51 (1963): 313-38.

7. Don L. Bosseau, "The Computer in Serials Processing and Control," in *Advances in Librarianship* (New York: Seminor Press, 1971).

8. U.S. President's Science Advisory Committee, *Scientific and Technological Communication in the Government* (Washington, D.C.: Government Printing Office, 1963).

13

9. U.S. President's Science Advisory Committee, *Improving the Availability of Scientific and Technical Information in the United States* (Washington, D.C.: Government Printing Office, 1968).

10. U.S. President's Science Advisory Committee, *Science, Government and Information: The Responsibilities of the Technical Community and the Government in the Transfer of Information* (Washington, D.C.: Government Printing Office, 1963).

11. Richard DeGennaro, "Wanted: A Minicomputer Serials Control System," *Library Journal* 102 (April 1977): 878-79.

12. Mary Sauer, "Automated Serials Control: Cataloging Considerations," *Journal of Library Automation* 9 (March 1976): 8-18.

13. Paul Fasana, "Serials Data Control: Current Problems and Prospects," *Journal of Library Automation* 9 (March 1976): 19-33.

14. Barbara Radke and Mike Berger. *Analysis of the 1977 University of California Union List of Serials* (Berkeley: Universitywide Library Automation Program, University of California, 1978).

15. J.E. Trent Reid, "CANUC Serials Reporting and the Canadian Mini-MARC Serials Holdings Format," *Serials Librarian* 3 (Spring 1979): 231-42.

16. American National Standards Institute, Committee Z39, Subcommittee 42. *Serial Holdings Statements at the Sensory Level.* (ANSI Z39.42 — 1980) New York: American National Standards Institute, 1980.

17. William J. Willmering, "On-Line Centralized Serials Control." *The Serials Librarian* 1 (Spring 1977): 243-49; James Fayollat, "On-Line Serials Control in a Large Biomedical Library: Part I. Description of the System." *Journal of the American Society for Information Science* 23 (September 1972): 318-22.

DISCUSSION

Velma Veneziano, Northwestern University: To what do you attribute the high cost of converting your serials records, $13 per title? The reason I question that is because we converted ours for a fraction of that.

Mr. Tonkery: I can explain that fairly well, I believe. The $13 is, in fact, an average figure. Many titles cost more than that. One of the commitments that we made when we undertook the conversion effort was that we would follow national standards. So as many records as possible are being converted to a full MARC record according to CONSER standards. If you are aware of the varying cataloging practices that have been buried in the card catalog, you must recognize that if you convert records and bring them into compliance with national standards for $13, you are ahead of the game.

Ms. Veneziano: So that cost includes both the conversion of records and the upgrading of the contents of those records to national standards.

Mr. Tonkery: Yes, and also the problem we encounter when the OCLC record says one thing and our local record says something else. Sometimes we find three local records in conflict with each other. The conversion cost includes reconciling these various records and arriving at one essentially standard record.

Berna Heyman, College of William and Mary: With the conversion, did you change your entries to successive entries as necessary.

Mr. Tonkery: We are following the CONSER standard. There is a date cut-off, I think it is 1965 or 1967, for successive entries, and we do add successive entries. Part of that is done by the conversion staff and part by the continuation department.

Frank Bright, University of Wisconsin: Dan, I would be interested in knowing if UCLA or any of the other libraries represented here have made any efforts to pick authenticated CONSER records as they become available and to substitute them for local cataloging in order to achieve this national standard bibliographic record that you talked about.

Mr. Tonkery: I don't know what other libraries are doing, but I know we are trying to build a database that has the highest quality record in it. Most of the time, that means that we would take the CONSER record of the CONSER member record unauthenticated. And many times it is in conflict with our own records, as you are probably well aware. We will accept the CONSER record and then go back to modify our records to conform to that. Accepting national standards is having an impact because the machine file is the replacement for the card catalog or at least for the serials part of the card catalog. So there is a great deal of inconsistency between the records that are in the machine and the records that are in the card catalog. At some point we will have to withdraw the records from the card catalog rather than go back and change the cards and go through that whole cycle.

Mr. Bright: I think you have answered my follow-up question, which was going to be the matter of the card catalog. You are allowing a discrepancy to continue, then, between your machine-readable records and the card catalog? You are not correcting the card catalog?

Mr. Tonkery: We are not correcting the card catalog for the most part.

Bob Holley, University of Utah: I am curious whether you believe that serials should be considered in a wider context as part of a totally integrated processing and retrieval system so that your serial database would also be your circulation database, your ordering database, and your online catalog. The serials system, then, would be just one part of either a turnkey or an in-house developed system, rather than being independent as I had the feeling you were describing in your talk.

Mr. Tonkery: Perhaps I didn't do justice to the UCLA system. It is an integrated system. I only talked about the serials aspect of it. In terms of circulation, we are on a turnkey circulation system which was selected by the university as a whole, so we cannot develop a local circulation system without getting into a great deal of difficulty since they control the budget. So our local system will include an online catalog, but not circulation at this point, and it is an integrated system.

Mr. Holley: I am sorry, I was talking more philosophically. You spoke of competition for resources among other priorities within the library. I would be much happier feeling that whatever I was doing now would indeed be compatible with the next building block that I would like to put in. So that in a certain sense it is not a competition but merely building a base, and at some point, either early or late, the serials module will fit in very nicely.

Mr. Tonkery: I think it will. As I said, I may not have done justice to the system because it does fit in with the acquisition system. If all your records are in a MARC format, they will intermesh. Whether you agree that MARC is a national standard or not is another matter.

Kaye Gapen, Iowa State University: From your experience in converting in a union list situation, can you give us advice about maintaining consistency of entry and holdings and the whole business? Do you have a central agency for conversion and quality control or is control decentralized? How have you been successful, if you feel you have?

Mr. Tonkery: That is a very difficult question. I think it is more a political question than it is a technical one, at least in a large campus environment where you have four cataloging centers and a conversion center. The conversion center is converting all records, which means they do law, they do bio-med, and they do many others. And you often get into a territorial dispute when the conversion center is trying to create one of the titles or convert one of the titles. If they make a decision to put it under successive entry, for example, catalogers from an area, say law or bio-med, may disagree. So you get into a political situation, and we have drawn up what is in fact a treaty. I say that in all honesty because it is a treaty. There has been some bloodshed here and there over territory involving what is the title, what title should be converted, how should it be converted, and what are the standards for that conversion. It is always the feeling that the conversion staff, because they are not ordained catalogers, are not doing an acceptable job in terms of the quality that most catalogers would require. However, once the information is loaded online, which we have done for all serials, the other cataloging centers can search that file and edit the entries. But we also have a treaty on what they can change and what they cannot change. But it is a problem, in a large environment. This problem is compounded because parallel conversion efforts are also being done at Berkeley and Stanford and we have some inconsistency in the records of these three institutions. The same title may be converted two different ways or three ways, with different choice and form of entry. Merging these records is an even more interesting problem.

Ms. Gapen: I have one follow-up question. Does your changing of entries and the treaty force you to rely on some sort of joint authority file? How do you handle your authority work in a conversion like that?

Mr. Tonkery: The conversion staff has a modified online authority file which they are using. For every record that they have been working with, they have created a cross-reference or authority file. There are about 15,000 records in that file. Unfortunately, that file may contain records or authorities that the catalog department has not established and has not used. When you are using the hybrid record, you know at many times that it has been submitted by a CONSER member. These records were developed under different authority conditions. So your record at the local campus starts to take on the complexion of other people's authority work and does not always represent the authority work done by the ordained centers, if you will. And so there is a problem of consistency in authority work. But that is controlled primarily with the projects having their own online authority system which they control and the catalogers still having the manual system. We try to work out some cross over of information.

Michael Gorman, University of Illinois: I have two questions for you, but before that I would like to congratulate you on recognizing the ordination of catalogers. Two questions, first you alluded to the difficulties of changes from later to successive entries and international standards and so on. You quote Paul Fasana who, of course, is against those changes. I would like to have your views on whether you think those changes are worth the trouble they cause? The second question is, do you really have a continuations department? A whole department just for continuations?

Mr. Tonkery: I will answer the second question first. Amira Lefkowitz, who is the head of the continuations department, is in the audience, and if I told you we didn't have a department, I would be in trouble. I guess there are six or seven people devoted to serials cataloging just within the university research library. So there is definitely a department dealing with that issue. Your recent writings have indicated that perhaps that is not necessary, but I haven't told those people that yet.

To respond to your other question relating to the international standards, I am prejudiced in my answer because I spent ten years at the National Library of Medicine, which is very interested in standards, and so perhaps I have a jaundiced view. I do support international standards, and I have requested that our staff follow international as well as national standards, and in doing so, recognizing that this adds to the cost. You know we could have converted serials for $5 per title had we decided not to use the MARC format, decided not to follow the CONSER editing guide, and decided not to follow the ANSI standards for holdings. We could have done our own thing, and we could have done it a lot cheaper. But we decided, why spend the $5 locally when that information couldn't be shared with anybody on an acceptable basis. We are trying to create a record which can be shared and which can be used by other libraries in order to save the expense of doing it themselves. That is part of the whole business of developing a national serials database. I think it is critical that if anybody else wants to do serials automation, they should be able to go to a database and use a record that they can have some degree of confidence in. You may not agree with everything, but at least you know what standards it has been subjected to. I think back to the early days of CONSER with OCLC and the MULS [Minnesota Union List of Serials] records and the PITT [University of Pittsburgh] records. I do not mean to malign them necessarily, but they were union list records which were somewhat skeletal and which caused a great deal of problems in terms of upgrading. So I think it is better essentially to bite the bullet and follow the standards. Certainly the international standards have been worth it, and I think they will facilitate the machine transmission in the exchange of information.

Irene Wernstedt, Pennsylvania State University: In discussing your conversion, you talk about the bibliographic holdings. Were you also converting your numerical and chronological holdings.

Mr. Tonkery: You are talking about the summary holdings?

Ms. Wernstedt: Did you use summary holdings?

Mr. Tonkery: Yes. We are following the ANSI standard as close as we can. We are doing that at the same time we are doing the processing of the bibliographic information and with the same personnel. We also have another group of staff that are collecting what I would call the processing information — bindery records, check-in, individual issues, subscription information — which is appended to that master record so that in one place you have full information regarding a particular serial title.

Online Serials Check-in at UCLA: A Design for the 1980s

JAMES E. FAYOLLAT

Serials check-in cannot be considered as an isolated activity since there are many integrated processes embedded in the check-in procedure. It is difficult to single out check-in per se for discussion without covering many ancillary design issues for serials control systems. Therefore, I have included several issues which will be of current interest. I will first give a short overview and historical perspective of check-in systems which will help define terms and set the stage for a discussion. Following the overview, I will briefly discuss serials online check-in in an operating environment at the UCLA Biomedical Library. I will conclude with a discussion of the generic design problems for a large online serials control system on a multi-library campus and explain how we have approached the problem at UCLA.

OVERVIEW AND HISTORICAL PERSPECTIVE

Traditionally, whether we are talking about a manual system, a non-online computer system, or an online system, the serials check-in process involves four major elements:

1. Identifying the serial, attempting to find a local record for it, and determining whether it should be checked in at this location.

James E. Fayollat is principal programmer at the University of California-Los Angeles Library

2. Recording the receipt of the piece in hand
3. Marking the issue as may be necessary, e.g., recording the call number and routing on the issue
4. Routing the issue to its next destination.

For most check-in operations there are at least two additional elements:

1. Initiation of claiming action for skipped issues
2. Initiation of bindery action for completed volumes.

Manual systems, as a practical matter, have no alternative but to use what has become known as the acceptance method of check-in. By this we mean that whatever issue is received is merely entered in the Kardex or other manual file.

Many of the earlier computer systems, such as those operated at the University of California-San Diego, Purdue University, Washington University, and others, were batch systems that depended upon keypunched cards. These systems used essentially an acceptance method of check-in. Either cards were keypunched after the issue arrived or the system may have generated a packet of cards from which selections could then be drawn. Several of the earlier systems developed online input mechanisms, but for the most part still remain as batch-oriented systems.

Early work at the UCLA Biomedical Library[1] and elsewhere aimed at establishing predictive patterns for serials from which could be derived some predictions about the expected arrival of issues. A feature common to these early keypunched card-oriented systems was the tub file which contained prepunched cards for the next expected issue of each serial. Some systems successfully varied this process by producing cards for all serials expected to arrive in the next time period, commonly one month.

Keypunched card-oriented predictive systems of this period necessitated the development of fairly complex batch programs. This was particularly true of those in which the design called for the integration of the check-in function with skipped issue claiming and bindery functions and which attempted manipulation of the holdings statement of the record. They also demanded entry of sufficient variables into the records to handle the wide variety of publication, numbering, and receipt patterns of serials and the development of a commonly agreed upon coding format for a

21

detailed holdings statement that lent itself to computer programmed manipulations. However, for the price paid in development and input, several advantages that were formerly not possible
accrued to these systems. For example, they are less error prone,
involve fewer redundant operations, and keep the pattern of description consistent with the publication pattern.

A constant problem in the design and programming of predictive systems is dealing with those serials which are not predictable.
This problem was not really met satisfactorily until the advent of
the online system.

Online Serials Control Development in the United States

The implementation of online serials control in this country
paralleled the development of third-generation computer equipment which provided advanced operating systems, time-sharing
computers, and more economical secondary storage.

While there were several hundred batch serials control systems
operating in the early 1970s, only a handful of online serials systems were developed and implemented. Even now in 1980, the
number of online serials systems reported in the literature is less
than ten. To date only two major online real-time integrated systems are operational. One system was developed at Northwestern
University[2] and the other at UCLA. These systems handle online
searching, maintenance, record creation, and support check-in,
claiming and binding operations, as well as the production of
numerous public service lists. In addition, one bibliographic utility
provides limited serials receipt support but has not implemented
the full range of serials functions and products.

While I do not wish to compare systems, I would like to discuss
the original UCLA Biomedical Library design which has been extensively reported in the literature since 1972.[3] Its major features
are:

1. A MARC-like record which, in addition to fairly standard
   bibliographic information, has several local processing fields
   which facilitate the check-in, claiming and bindery modules, and associated products
2. A completely permuted title index, together with auxiliary indexes by subject, language, country, and ISSN, all of
   which may be accessed and manipulated with Boolean logic
3. An alphabetically ordered file which greatly facilitates

such operations as production of lists and alphabetically ordered search operations at the terminal.

4. Updating operations that are performed online via CRT terminals. Many of the check-in, claiming, and binding operations are preprogrammed to function automatically with minimum activity required on the part of the terminal operator.

The processing fields include the following data:

1. A detailed holdings statement
2. Fixed fields which contain:
   A. The expected year, volume, and issue information for the next issue to arrive if this information is predictable, as it is in over 70 percent of all serials
   B. Data which will assist the programs in the prediction process, including pattern of publication code, first and last issue of the volume, frequency, interval of receipt this year, and issues per volume
   C. The last issue received and its date of arrival
   D. Data for claiming and binding action which may be triggered by the check-in process
3. Various note fields such as those for claiming, binding, supplement issues, etc.

The key to the predictive aspect of the check-in system is the pattern code, a number from one to seventeen created in the original Biomedical Library system. The pattern code relates to such things as whether the issue numbering is present and, if so, whether it is continuous or repeating and whether it is numeric or otherwise (e.g., season or month).

Briefly, the online serials check-in process is as follows. Once the program has been switched to the check-in operation, the retrieval of a record in the system will display what we call a check-in line, followed below by selected fields from the record. The check-in line in most cases will show the year, volume, issue number, and date of the piece to be checked-in. If this information matches the piece in hand, all that is needed is for the operator to depress the transmit key. At this time the program will add the issue to the holdings statement using character manipulation algorithms, check for possible skipped issue and/or binding actions that may be required, and finally generate the next expected issue

23

information. The operator can verify the correctness of all actions taken by the program immediately and before any permanent update of the record is made.

It will sometimes be the case that certain information is not predictable, or the publication pattern may change, or a number of other things may occur which will necessitate some keying onto the CRT by the check-in assistant. This is normally a straightforward process for the operator after some training. The predictive features of the system are not always used. For example, if a serial's identification and description of issue received is so unusual that it cannot be adequately handled with the predictive algorithms, then the receipt can be entered as in an acceptance system, i.e., by keying the appropriate data into the holdings or other appropriate field.

A more detailed description of the check-in, claiming, and binding activities of the UCLA serials system will be covered later. At this time I will expand my discussion from basic check-in related matters to more general design concepts and problems.

ENHANCEMENT OF THE BIOMEDICAL LIBRARY SYSTEM FOR THE UCLA CAMPUS

During the planning phase for the automation of technical services on the UCLA campus, we began to give serious consideration to the enhancement of the biomedical online serials control system for the UCLA Campus Library network approximately one year ago. As of today we have over 25,000 serials records online which have the full complement of Marc bibliographic data present on the OCLC archive tapes and about 29,000 minimum level records which are a product of our "Current Serials Title List" project in an auxiliary online file. Full-level records are being added to the OCLC-Marc file at the rate of about 1,200 per month, the data coming in from OCLC's subscription service. These records are a product of our Title II-C serials conversion grant and the output of our four cataloging centers.

The major design issues involved in the enhancement project included:

1. *File size implications.* The Biomedical Library had about

7,500 active serials titles and a similar number of dead titles. What are the problems in taking a system originally designed for a data base of this size and using the software to support a library network of some twenty branches and a total number of live titles exceeding 55,000 titles? Could we operate with one large file or would we have to be content with several smaller local files?

2. *Increased terminal load.* What are the technical aspects of computer capacity and design aspects of the software program which potentially could limit the system to just a few terminals? What are the problems in increasing from five terminals to over thirty in the serials area?

3. *Database security.* How could we guarantee the integrity of the file with multiple libraries accessing and updating bibliographic and processing information? Would we be able to maintain control over such aspects of the file as integrity of the filing order of the records in alphabetical order, and authority control over the bibliographic data? What about security and access between different library units in general?

4. *Record structure.* Could the original design be modified to accommodate a full MARC format including indicators, repeating fields, subfields, etc.? Would major modifications need to be made to our internal processing format?

5. *Boolean searching capability.* What would happen to our searching module when it began dealing with so many records? Would we have to revert to some sort of search code scheme and do away with our permuted title and Boolean logic?

6. *System limitations.* In general, what major enhancements, if any, would be necessary that might call for a complete redesign of the system? Should we, for example, redesign the system for a minicomputer?

These and other questions called for a design philosophy and myriad decisions. Without attempting to specifically answer each of these questions in turn, I will direct my discussion to the major problems we faced and how they were resolved. I would first like to mention briefly the hardware, software, and physical environment and then discuss the interface with OCLC as it pertains to the development of the serials database.

25

Environment

The UCLA Library Technical Processing System uses the UCLA office of Academic Computing (OAC) Facility's IBM 3033 computer. This is a large campus research computer, currently configured with 12 million bytes of online memory, and with a rated speed of approximately 4.5 million instructions per second. The library's application program operates under TSO (time-sharing option). Programming and job submittal are generally done under Wylbur, a generalized text-editing and job submittal system supported by the OAC computer. All programs are written in PL/1. The online system uses approximately eighty program modules, which average on the order of 300 instructions each. The batch support programs approximate the number and size of the online modules.

The data management of the system employs our own program code only. That is, the system does not make use of any generalized data base management system, such as IBM's VSAM. However, it should be pointed out that our local code duplicates to a large extent the various features of VSAM and performs additional indexing functions that VSAM is unable to perform. A design problem which we will probably have to address in a year or so is that the terminal management system, running as it does under TSO, does not provide for reentrant program code as would a transaction-oriented system like IBM's CICS (Customer Information Control System). Therefore, each terminal using the system, at least for now, must use its own copy of the online program module. It remains to be seen how many simultaneous terminals we can put on the computer system before this becomes a real problem. We now have as many as ten and before long will expand to approximately thirty.

As has already been mentioned, the library has twenty branches and four processing centers. One of the goals of the new system is to decentralize processing over a period of time as much as seems feasible. This decentralization will be facilitated with the installation of terminals in the various branches to retrieve and update records.

File Structure and Contents

The new system contains all the bibliographic data of the full MARC communications format, and thus the length and complexity of the serials records in the file have been significantly increased from the original design. Adherence to national and international standards, such as MARC, the ANSI standards for holdings statements, and *AACR,* allows us to share our data with the bibliographic utilities, the University of California's bibliographic center, the Division of Library Automation, as well as to participate in other cooperative projects which might arise.

Full indexing and Boolean search access is supported for several fields in the record, including all 1xx (author), 2xx (title) fields, the 260 $a subfield (place of publication), the 710 (added entry), the OCLC number, record number, ISSN, etc. The addition of records to the file, as well as changes to records which may add or modify indexed fields, invoke program modules which dynamically modify the index files, thus keeping them current at all times.

OCLC Interface

The UCLA Library uses OCLC heavily. Each week an OCLC subscription tape arrives from Columbus containing an average of over 2,000 bibliographic records. Programs have been written to convert these records to our processing format, select them for addition to either the MARC serials file or the online monograph archive file, and do the necessary processing for loading them into the respective files. This process is fairly sophisticated and merits some discussion.

Central to our design philosophy is the decision to always maintain all of our files, both serials and monograph, in main entry filing order. This is accomplished by several programs. The first step in the process is to create a string of up to 144 characters that can be used to collate the record in the proper main entry filing order. This main entry sort field is constructed from the MARC 1xx author fields and the 245 field (or, if there is no 1xx field, just the 245 field). When the file is in ascending order by this main entry sort field which is prefixed to the front of the record, the file is in correct filing order.

Perhaps the most sophisticated step of the weekly OCLC merge process is the actual online loading and simultaneous indexing of the records into the online files. The large online file of serials records is in alphabetical order, each record having a prefix of up to 144 characters which orders the record in the file.

Each record to be loaded is treated precisely as if it were a new record created at the terminal and is moved into the master file in the proper alphabetical order. The program creates all of the necessary indexes for the record, updating the index (or dictionary) file dynamically as it goes.

This "dynamic move" process is currently done online. Because of this, any problems which may occur in the process can be analyzed at the time of occurrence and appropriate action taken. Also, the process merely puts into a loop the program modules which are invoked whenever any record is added online, or for that matter when any record already existing in the master file is altered in such a manner that it must be repositioned in a new sequential order in the file. This process should be examined more closely since it involves some important space management considerations.

Space Management

Perhaps one of the most difficult challenges faced by the designer of a dynamically updatable online system is that of overcoming the limitations imposed by the fixed length of a disk track. We have solved the problem of updating variable length records online with the following space management technique.

When a file is loaded onto a disk, the program leaves some slack space on each track and does not allow a record to be split over two tracks. On every few tracks additional slack space is allocated. The online programs which modify records, facilitate creation of new records, and perform the "dynamic move" routine for weekly records from OCLC can either find space on the desired track or can move records around within a few tracks until space is obtained to perform the record update or addition as desired. The alphabetical sequence is always maintained.

It was mentioned that the alphabetic sort prefix is retained in two places — first, in the front of the records themselves, and second, in the dictionary. Since the records are always maintained in alphabetical order, one may wonder why the sort prefix is also in the dictionary. The reason is that it greatly facilitates the determination of where a new record, whether from the new entry routines, or from the "dynamic move" routines, is to go in the main file. It is a relatively simple process to take the new record's alphabetic prefix and search for it, or more likely, a close match, in the dictionary, obtain the internal record number of a record

28

that will be close to the correct place for the new record, and then use that number to ascertain the correct master file disk track to read so that the final placement and assignment of the internal record number of the new record can occur.

Security

Access to the system is via seven-character passwords which users enter during the log-on process. If the system does not recognize the password, it will deny access to the person trying to log on. The system tallies each use of a password and records the duration of use.

One or more commands may be executed automatically upon recognition of the password to preset the program to the usual operations desired by that user. Thus, the system will point the user to the file he wants to be in and set the appropriate function switches. These default commands can also be overridden with supplied commands if desired.

The password is used to supply information to the system with regard to two major types of authorizations. These two categories of authorizations are (1) whether or not the user has permission to update files, and if so, which files; and (2) which fields he may update. For example, a user may be allowed to have search capability only, or to be able to update one of the files listed as updatable for that password, or to have the ability to update any file in the system. Similarly, a user may be allowed to update her own branch fields only, or one of the branches in a list, or any field in the record. Branched fields will be discussed below.

Every file in the system has an access code which designates whether that file is updatable, searchable only, or locked. If the file is locked, access to the file for searching or updating is denied unless the user also provides a second access code, called a key, which matches the lock code. If the file is designated as searchable only, unrestricted access is permitted, but with search capability only.

Branched Fields

An important design objective of the new Technical Processing System was to eliminate the duplication of bibliographic records in the system, thus creating a single database for the entire campus library network. We have achieved this goal by designing a record which, in addition to containing bibliographic fields, contains local processing fields (called "branched fields") which may repeat as necessary for the branches holding the items. The files for the UCLA serials and acquisitions systems employ the branched field concept for approximately twenty fields of local processing information in the locally assigned 9xx fields.

In a MARC record certain fields, such as subject fields, may be repeated. The concept of branched fields takes this process a step farther and makes a given field not only repeatable but also repeatable by branch library designation. For example, the local holdings field could be repeated several times, once for each branch library which has issues of that journal. Additionally, within a branch, if more than one copy is held, the local holdings field could be repeated for each copy.

The directory of the record contains bits which specify ownership of a field by a branch. While the MARC communications format uses a repeating 12-character directory for each field or tag, our internal processing format uses only four characters for each directory entry, and the values are stored in binary. Two characters are a binary starting position. The other two contain the tag value and branch value. The system provides for up to 63 branch designations and a tag which may have a value from 0001 through 1027. Tag values of 1000 and above are designated as hidden fields and are normally updatable only under program control. Two such fields are now in use. One records a history of recent updates to the record, indicating the date, process, and user who updated the record. The other keeps a chronological history of the creation of branched fields in the record.

On the CRT screen nonbranched fields (the bibliographic fields) appear with the branch notation "<00>." Branched fields appear with a two-letter mnemonic notation such as "<LW>." The mnemonic notation is the code for a branch library in the system. "LW," for example, could designate the law library. The translation of the binary value in the record's directory (which uses six bits) to the mnemonic is achieved with a table in the program.

As stated previously, the security code can specify that a given user may have permission to update only specified branches. Actually, the rules are slightly more complex. For example, if one or more branches are represented in the record that are not in the list of updatable branches associated with the security code, then the user also cannot update any of the bibliographic data fields. However, if only the user's branch or set of branches are represented in the record, then the user is permitted to update the bibliographic fields.

The guidelines described above for authorizing the update of specific fields apply also to functions such as serials check-in. For example, a user can check in issues for any branch for which the user is authorized and can see the holdings of other branches, but not update or check-in for other branches. In this regard, the system has been designed to provide for a large variety of display needs. For example, the user may want to see all holdings of all branches, or of a specified branch or list of branches. The user may want to see only specific bibliographic fields and all processing fields. Provision is made for a very flexible approach to these needs.

Summary of Design Problems

To summarize, the principal problems of enhancing the UCLA Biomedical Library system to serve a large campus network have been met by a combination of better technology and programming sophistication. While we probably could have used minicomputer technology, we have chosen instead to use our large campus computer with its powerful processing and terminal support capabilities. We have successfully achieved an interface with OCLC in the development of our dynamic move operation which loads records online completely indexed within hours of receipt of the OCLC tapes. File size, in terms of the number of records stored and updated and in terms of our Boolean searching algorithms, has proven to be a manageable problem, again due to a combination of better technology in the form of online disks of enormous capacity and more advanced database design enhancements. Finally, database security issues have been met with our branched field concept, permitting multiple access to records which combine bibliographic and local processing data.

The original check-in operation, designed over ten years ago, remains largely unchanged as a viable component of the online system. I will conclude with a summary of the check-in process under the enhanced system and a brief description of the essential aspects of the claiming and bindery operations.

James E. Fayollat

SUMMARY OF THE AUTOMATED SERIALS
CHECK-IN PROCESS

The following steps summarize the check-in process at UCLA:

1. The check-in assistant logs on with an authorization number which will preset the program to look only for currently received serials. The authorization will also preset the screen display and program for the check-in task. If the authorization is for a single location only, such as a branch library, the program will be preset to display that library's holdings and check-in screens first for any serials which are held in multiple locations.

2. The check-in assistant will next search for the serial in hand. Searches can be conducted by various words in the entry or by the ISSN if it should appear on the issue. When the record is displayed on the screen, the check-in assistant verifies that it is for the correct title and the appropriate copy. This can be determined from the holdings display and location and routing codes in the case of multiple copies within the same branch.

3. If the issue in hand is the next predicted one, the check-in assistant need only transmit a single command to the computer. If it is not the expected issue, two possibilities arise: (a) if it is a future issue, the check-in assistant will key any differences over the predicted issue and will transmit that to the computer, and a "skipped issue" claim note will be generated by the program; or (b) if it is a back issue which has arrived, the operator will key it directly into the holdings statement and clear the outstanding claim note. Prompting commands for check-in appear at appropriate stages. Error messages will also be generated if the check-in assistant does not perform the check-in operation properly. The check-in record carries routing instructions and any special handling information. The check-in assistant can use this to route the issues to the appropriate shelving location within the library.

   Claiming: In addition to skipped issue claiming, there are several additional methods of claiming. Records may contain a "months to claim" code assigned on the basis of frequency and country of origin, which represents the

32

number of months allowed to elapse before overdue claiming is initiated. Another code is used for issuing requests for renewal. If a vendor does not accept subscriptions for a serial, this code is the calendar month of the year in which a reauthorization letter is sent out requesting the next issue. There are also codes which may indicate that it is especially important for a serial to be claimed or that it should not be claimed.

In the serials claiming module, online operations exist for various categories of claims. The actual generation of the claim letters is initiated by a claiming assistant who systematically reviews the titles flagged for claiming and makes the decision as to whether or not a claim should be issued. An overnight batch run then produces claim letters for selected items. At the time the claim is produced by the program, a code in the claim processing field is changed automatically to show the letter has actually been generated.

Binding: When the first issue of a new volume or binding unit arrives, the serial is flagged to indicate that the previous unit should be bound. The serial unit scheduled for binding will appear on a computer-generated pickup list which is used to notify the binding assistant to pull issues from the shelves. If the issues are complete, the pickup code is changed to one which on the overnight batch run will print bindery slips. The program then changes the code to show the slip has been printed. Packing lists are also generated from this program for shipments to the bindery. If issues are incomplete, the title will appear on future lists for additional searches on the shelves, or codes can be changed to indicate a replacement order is required if the issue is considered to be permanently missing after several searches on the shelves.

When a volume is returned from the bindery the binding assistant has two options: (a) a code can be changed in the binding field which will clear the at bindery information and automatically update the bound part of the holdings statement; or (b) the holdings can be updated directly by keying, and the bindery note deleted by the assistant.

Since the check-in, claiming, and bindery modules are all interrelated in the system, the bound and unbound holdings should always reflect the current processing activity. Public lists generated from the system include complete holdings statements, including notes on the date of the last receipt of an issue, and all outstanding claiming and binding activity.

CONCLUSION

Technological advances which have produced faster, more reliable computers with easy access through modern online communication techniques have made feasible online library systems such as the one just described. The programs for such a system, while complex and requiring years of development effort, have actually become more manageable due to the availability of new programming tools and processing techniques.

Building on our existing online real-time system at UCLA, it has been possible to develop a multi-library check-in system using a full MARC record as the base record. The base record is obtained from OCLC, reformatted for local processing, and added online with a dynamic move operation that inserts the record alphabetically into the master file and builds all the indexing for Boolean searching.

Large real-time online serials check-in systems are feasible based on current technology. There is little reason to wait for new technological advances.

REFERENCES

1. D. Bishop; A. L. Milner, and F. W. Roper, "Publication Patterns of Scientific Serials," *American Documentation* 16 (1965): 113-22; James E. Fayollat, "On-Line Serials Control in a Large Biomedical Library: Part II, Evaluation of Retrieval Features," *Journal of the American Society for Information Science* 23 (Nov.-Dec. 1972): 353-58.

2. William J. Willmering, "On-Line Centralized Serials Control," *Serials Librarian* 1 (Spring 1977): 243-49.

3. Louise Darling and James E. Fayollat, "Evolution of a Processing System in a Large Biomedical Library," *Bulletin of the Medical Library Association* 64 (Jan. 1976): 20-24; James E. Fayollat, *Technical Processing System Procedures and Documentation Manual: On-line Serials and Cataloging Modules* (Los Angeles: Biomedical Library, University of California, 1976);

idem, "On-Line Serials Control at UCLA," *Proceedings of the 1972 Clinic on Library Applications of Data Processing.* (Urbana: University of Illinois Graduate School of Library Science, 1972), pp. 69-81; idem, "On-Line Serials Control in a Large Biomedical Library: Part I, Description of the System," *Journal of the American Society for Information Science* 23 (Sept.-Oct. 1972): 318-22; idem, "On-Line Serials Control in a Large Biomedical Library: Part II, Evaluation of Retrieval Features," *Journal of the American Society for Information Science* 23 (Nov.-Dec. 1972): 353-58; idem, "On-Line Serials Control in a Large Biomedical Library: Part III, Comparison of On-Line and Batch Operations and Cost Analysis," *Journal of the American Society for Information Science* 24 (Mar.-Apr. 1973): 80-86; Fred W. Roper, "A Computer-Based Serials Control System for a Large Biomedical Library," *American Documentation* 19 (1968): 151-57.

DISCUSSION

John Parkhari, Canadian Institute for Scientific and Technical Information: How long does it take to check in a particular issue?

Mr. Fayollat: That can vary a great deal. It could be anywhere from less than one-half minute to quite a long time depending on whether there are problems with the issue. What we have done, to some extent, is have the check-in assistants do as much check-in as possible, setting aside any problems which might occur for a supervisor to examine later. Typical daily production is on the order of what you would do with a manual cardex. You can do about sixty an hour; about one a minute on average.

Jim Linderman, Upjohn Company: My question is not really related to the system design, but rather how it is used. I wondered if you have found that publishers and vendors are receptive to fulfilling computer-generated claims requests and whether the success rate has ever been analyzed. We throw away hundreds of computerized invoices from publishers. I wondered if they are doing the same.

Mr. Fayollat: I would prefer to have one of my colleagues from UCLA answer that question.

Lelde Gilman, UCLA: We have been using the system for ten years. We send a claim letter which tells the vendor which volume or issue is missing and leaves them space to answer why it is missing — whether it has not yet been published and so forth. Most of the vendors that we have dealt with over a period of time will do exactly what the letter says. Sometimes they may attach their own reply to it, but they will return our letter, which we ask them to do because it includes our control number.

Mark Kibbey, Columbia University: I would like to address the point from the gentleman from Upjohn. I used to be with Institute for Scientific Information, and ISI has an online serials system which is at least as integrated and as online as the two mentioned by the speaker, although it has not been discussed in the literature because ISI has been thinking about making it commercially available. But the point is that you can tie an automated system into your word processing system and come out with claims, notices, etc., that are much less mechanical looking than the usual sort of thing that you fill out from a typical cardex. In fact, you can very much improve your output for claims and the look of it and responses to it.

Mr. Fayollat: Thank you. That is a good thought. We have not done that.

Esther Greenberg, Case Western Reserve University: Could you be a little more specific about how you handle the unpredictable titles? I think I missed something there.

Mr. Fayollat: I mentioned the check-in line. The line has room for filling in the year, the volume, the issue, the date on the issue if it's available, and other information that would be integrated into the holdings statement by the program modules. Now, for many journals, not all those items that I mentioned are predictable. For example, you might know that the next issue will use the next successive number, but you do not know for sure what year it will appear. So when you call up the record, the screen will be blank in the year portion and there will normally be a message on the screen that says "Please fill in the year" because it is not available. So you just type in the year on the terminal. One could say that predictable elements are not that critical to the design of the system. They facilitate many of the operations that otherwise would have to be keyed in on the screen.

Joan Butler, University of Wisconsin, Milwaukee: My question concerns your system's integration with OCLC. Specifically, when you get the archive tapes, they include items that have been recataloged or the bibliographic description has been revised in some way. What process is used in your system to get that revised data into your system? And then, what are the channels of communication between the people doing the check-in, say, who would first notice a title change?

Mr. Fayollat: That has not been completely implemented. Until recently, we have not been adding any local processing data. And so, when one of those replacement records came in, it would completely replace the existing record. That will not be possible in the future system. In the short run the answer, from a design perspective, is that those new records will not be permitted to update the old records. In the longer run, I'm sure programs will be written to replace just those fields which are permitted to be replaced. I'm sure there will be a listing and other kinds of notifications printed as a result of this online process that people will have to look through and decide to do a local update to the local file or whatever. I think another answer to that is that we will discourage going to OCLC just to make a change when it can be made locally more easily and cheaply. If the purpose is to update the OCLC bibliographic record for CONSER or whatever, that is one thing, but if the purpose is just to update the OCLC record then so it can come back and update our record, we will discourage that or forbid it perhaps. Those things all are going to be worked out over the coming months. They are not all resolved.

Nancy Gonta, University of Maryland: With the unpredictable items, when you're not sure of the date or the frequency it's coming out, how are you handling the claiming mechanism? I have a second question. You said that the human operator is reviewing the claims online. How does that work? Do they ever get a print-out so they can double check human error or determine if something got missed or that something should not be claimed at this time? How is that being handled? Is it totally online?

Mr. Fayollat: You recall that I mentioned something called a month-to-claim code. For example, if a title is fairly unpredictable and it comes from India or some place, maybe the month-to-claim code will be set to eight months, which means we will wait eight months before we attempt to claim it. Now what happens is that you have checked it in on, let's say, January 1. Well, when you do this online reviewing, the record will not show up until after the first of August when you do your reviewing then. You will still make a judgment at that time. There are also note fields which you may choose to put in the record.

There is actually no way to program for more unpredictable issues because they are, by definition, unpredictable. So you provide links or hooks in the system that will permit the people to do the best they can. And I'm sure there will be room for design improvements in this area.

In answer to your other question, once the letters are produced it is dependent upon the person who is in charge of doing the stuffing and mailing as to whether they will go through those letters on a last minute basis or whatever. There is a title log produced, but as a practical matter, once the letter is produced it is mailed in the next couple of days. If there's a mistake, well, there's a mistake. That's it. I might say on this claiming matter, I have always been amazed at how many letters we send out. We send out a lot of letters. As Mrs. Gilman said, vendors respond pretty well. Better than you might think.

Kenton Andersen, Northwestern University: My question relates to the format of your records. Apparently, you have put all the holdings information for all the branches in one record.

Mr. Fayollat: That's correct.

Mr. Andersen: Do you have a problem with the records becoming too large to handle efficiently?

Mr. Fayollat: Well, we hope not. I set a limit of about 8,000 characters per record, and we will see if it starts getting up there. If you have, say, *Scientific American,* which might be received by three or four of your branches and maybe some of those have two or three copies, I could see how the records could grow to thousands of characters pretty quickly, because a lot of your bibliographic MARC records are a thousand or more. We are hoping that this will not be a problem and we will tackle it if it does.

Sally Voth, Kansas State University: What was the driving force for the elaborate security design?

Mr. Fayollat: Librarians. We had different people who said they wanted this and this and this and we tried to program to suit them. I am sure there will be more and more elaborations as the years go by. If it had been up to me, I would not have done it all. But that's the way they wanted it.

Kirk Memmott, Brigham Young University: As you know, we have patterned our system after the one you have developed. I find myself wanting to respond to all these questions, but I will not. My question has to do with timing, and it is more of a philosophical question than a technical question. You mentioned that technically the time is right to move into this sort of thing. Philosophically, however, considering all the developments by vendors, by some of the networks and so on, and considering the possibility of doing some local development, how would you proceed if you were a serials librarian?

Mr. Fayollat: Well, I have a hard time answering that question. My perspective is that of the designer of the system of UCLA. I can't give you any answer to what people around the country should attempt to do, except to say that it takes years and years to develop a system like this. These programs have been massaged and added to and manipulated, and they are continuing to be worked on at an ever increasing rate it seems. It is horribly expensive. Dan Tonkery mentioned earlier this morning that just to add the record to the file is also expensive. There are enough existing systems that a library that doesn't have the necessary funds certainly should look at what does exist and could save several hundred thousand dollars of effort.

Inventory and Holdings Features of Serials Control

SUSAN L. MILLER

Serials make up a major portion of published materials and are indispensable in the support and furtherance of research and study. Thus, for a library, especially a large research library, to be of service to its users, it must effectively handle the difficult problems of acquiring and processing serials and then making them available. These views are not new. They were expressed in the 1945 and 1946 annual reports of the Librarian of Congress. The fact that we are still wrestling with the problems of serials control thirty-five years later is an indication of why this topic is included in this institute.

The aspects of computer-assisted serial holdings control which will be covered in this paper include holdings notation, routing of newly received serial pieces, binding of completed volumes, and circulation of bound volumes.

HOLDINGS NOTATION

An examination of the approaches taken by two computer-based circulation systems to automating serials holdings will help define the problems involved in holdings notation. In both of these systems, the identification of the item to be loaned used the call number, copy number, and volume number. And in both systems, which were designed before 1970, volume numbers were placed in fixed length fields.

Susan L. Miller is coordinator of library automation at Ohio State University.

The first system at Queen's University Library, Kingston, Ontario, had four six-character fields available for the volume identification. The six characters was generous. However, once in a while, the field would be insufficient. For example, the word "appendix" will not fit into a single six-character field. Also, four fields are sometimes insufficient for volume identification. For example, the volume identified by series B, volume 3, part 2, pages 1-365, 1978, requires six of these fields according to conversion instructions for that system.

The second system, the original Library Circulation System (LCS), allowed only three numeric characters to identify a volume. This field was adequate only when all of the following conditions were met: (1) the number of volumes was less than 999; (2) all physical volumes were bound to match the bibliographic volume; (3) the publisher did not issue volumes in bibliographic parts such as part 1 and part 2; (4) no supplements, appendices, etc., were published; (5) the year was not used as the numbering scheme; (6) no new series, second series, etc., were present; (7) no volumes were identified with alphabetic characters. Needless to say, the three-character volume field was a failure from the beginning.

Experiences with these two systems emphasized the importance of

1. The holdings fields accepting variable length data
2. The display of holdings being clear to untrained users
3. Having more information on serial holdings patterns in order to design holdings fields for serials.

In 1972, the Ohio State University (OSU) Libraries Research and Development Division performed two rudimentary surveys of serial volume identification. In a survey on the total length of the volume identification, we learned that 11 percent of the volumes required three characters for identification, 30 percent of the volumes required four characters, and 50 percent required seven or fewer characters. The maximum length of the volume identification found was nineteen characters. In the second survey, the labeling instructions for bound serial volumes were studied. It was found that year was the enumeration for 39 percent of the serial titles examined, volume was the beginning enumeration for 40 percent of the titles, and number was the beginning enumeration for 17 percent of the titles. The remaining 4 percent of the titles began the enumeration with a series number.

The most detailed information on serial publication patterns available to date is an article by Grosch published in *Serial Librarian* in 1977.[1] In this analysis, she identifies three components of a holdings statement: (1) the natural language identifier, such as the word "volume" associated with the element of the number or issue identification scheme; (2) the issue identification data, which is usually numeric although alphanumeric or text data, such as "special issue," — may be encountered; and (3) the associated date of publication. She further states that in some cases the date is the only component of a holdings statement, and in other cases the date is completely missing.

In further analysis of the natural language identifier, Grosch identified forty-eight term patterns present in English, French, German, Scandinavian, Latin, and Russian serial publications. These term patterns have from one to six hierarchical levels. Examples of term pattern include volume subdivided by number or series divided by volume and part (see table 1). Grosch ends her article with an appeal for "further research into the holding statement aspect of serials system and database design."

In 1975, the American National Standard's Committee on Library and Information Sciences and Related Publishing Practices, Z39, appointed the Subcommittee on Serial Holdings Statements at the Summary Level. Under the chairmanship of Glyn T. Evans, this subcommittee has completed its work, and the *American National Standard for Serial Holdings Statements at the Summary Level* (ANSI Z39.42-1980) was issued in midsummer 1980. Quoting from the foreword, "This standard defines the data elements to be included by libraries, information centers, and other institutions when they record and report serial holdings to union lists."[2] The "standard" provides three levels for data reporting: level one includes institution, sublocation identifier, and copy number; level two builds on level one and includes additional mandatory fields of the date the report was made, a code specifying completeness of holdings, an acquisition status code, and a non-retention code; level three builds on levels one and two and includes ranges of enumeration (volume data) and chronology (date data). The standard states that holdings are to "be reported at the first-order designator level, for example year (but not month or day) . . . ."[3] The work of this subcommittee does not provide the answers for serial holdings control for circulation and bindery purposes. For this, standards for detailed holdings, for identifying individual volumes and issues are required.

A second ANSI Z39 subcommittee, chaired by Ann Ekstrom, was appointed in 1979. Quoting from the appointment letter, the subcommittee is "to prepare a draft standard dealing with publication patterns and their use in serials control. The specific purpose of the standard is to define a way of denoting the pattern of publication . . . . The scope of the subcommittee's efforts include the specifications of a procedure for the unambiguous encoding of publication patterns, definition of the codes to be employed, and specification and definition of the content designators for fields 330 and 331 of the MARC serials format."[4]

Also in 1979, a third ANSI Z39 subcommittee, chaired by Susan Brynteson, was appointed to design a standard for detailed holdings statements. The charge to the subcommittee identified eleven subtasks, some of these are covering all cases where the use of serial holdings is necessary, providing for holdings at the most specific level, providing for both bibliographic and physical units, allowing for the automatic derivation of summary holdings statements, accommodating automated and manual systems, and addressing the matter of piece level identification.[5]

Another development in the area of holdings statements is the IFLA-Unesco contract with Jean Whiffen, serials librarian at the University of Victoria Library in British Columbia. The title of the project is "UNESCO/IFLA Union List Project." Aspects of the project which may be helpful in local serial systems are the analysis of data records and record structure and the selection of essential data elements.[6]

The recommendations which develop in the previously mentioned projects are important considerations for the design of new systems which include serial holdings. The systems which will be described later were, for the most part, operational before any work on holdings notations standards.

DESIGN OF HOLDINGS FILES

After these rather brief comments on plans for standardizing holdings notation, there are a group of questions which must be considered before designing a serial holdings capability.

First, shall the holdings notation standard be adopted? The primary reason for adopting the national standards is to facilitate data sharing for union lists of holdings, etc. If the standard is not adopted for the system being planned, the holdings notation

Susan L. Miller

Table I *Term Pattern Table for English, French, German, Scandinavian,*

Term Pattern Number	Term Level A	Abbr.	Term Level B	Abbr.	Term Level C	Abbr.
01	Volume*	Vol.	Issue (No.)	No.	Part	Pt.
02	Series	Ser.	Volume*	Vol.	Issue (No.)	No.
03	Series	Ser.	Volume*	Vol.	Part	Pt.
04	Series	Ser.	Volume*	Vol.	Part	Pt.
05	Series	Ser.	Volume*	Vol.	Page	Pg.
06	Series	Ser.	Section*	Sec.	Volume	Vol.
07	Series	Ser.	Number*	No.		
08	Series	Ser.	Part*	Pt.		
09	Year*	Yr.	Quarter	Qtr.	Number	No.
10	Section	Sec.	Volume*	Vol.	Issue (No.)	No.
11	Quarter	Qtr.	Year*	Yr.	Number	No.
12	Year*	Yr.	Part	Pt.	Number	No.
13	Year*	Yr.	Section	Sec.	Paper No.	PNo.
14	Session	Ses.	Volume*	Vol.		
15	Volume*	Vol.	:	:	:	:
16	Part	Pt.	Volume*	Vol.		
17	Number*	No.	Part	Pt.		
18	Auflage	Auf.	Band*	Bd.	Teil	T.
19	Band*	Bd.	Abteilung	Abt.	Buch	Bch.
20	Band*	Bd.	Abteilung	Abt.	Buch	Bch.
21	Band*	Bd.	Abteilung	Abt.	Buch	Bch.
22	Band*	Bd.	Abteilung	Abt.	Halft(e)	Hal.
23	Band*	Bd.	Abteilung	Abt.	Lieferung	Lfg.
24	Band*	Bd.	Abteilung	Abt.	Teil	T.
25	Band*	Bd.	Bogen	Bog.		
26	Band*	Bd.	Halft(e)	Hal.	Lieferung	Lfg.
27	Band*	Bd.	Halft(e)	Hal.	Teil	T.
28	Band*	Bd.	Heft	Hft.	Bogen	Bog.
29	Band*	Bd.	Heft	Hft.	Teil	T.
30	Band*	Bd.	Lieferung	Lfg.	Bogen	Bog.
31	Band*	Bd.	Lieferung	Lfg.	Seite	St.
32	Band*	Bd.	Part	Pt.		
33	Band*	Bd.	Teil	T.	Bandteil	BdT.
34	Jahr*	Jar.	Heft	Hft.		
35	Lieferung*	Lfg.				
36	Pars*	Par.	Teil	T.		
37	Part*	Pt.	Bilaga	Bil.		
38	Part*	Pt.	Teil	T.		
39	Page	Pg.	Page (cont.)	Pg.		
40	Volume*	Vol.	Band	Bd.	Teil	T.
41	Volume*	Vol.	Fasicule	Fas.		
42	Volume*	Vol.	Heft	Hft.		
43	Seriia	Ser.	Tom*	Tom	Vypchsk	Vyp.
44	Tom*	Tom	Vypchsk	Vyp.	Chast	Cha.
45	Volume*	Vol.	Part	Pt.	Tom	Tom
46	Volume*	Vol.	Tom	Tom	Vypchsk	Vyp.
47	Heft*	Hft.				
48						
.						
.						
99						

44

Latin, and Russian Languages

Term Level D	Abbr.	Term Level E	Abbr.	Term Level F	Abbr.
Page	Pg.	Page (cont.)	Pg.		
Part	Pt.	Page	Pg.	Page (cont.)	Pg.
Page	Pg.	Page (cont.)	Pg.		
Fasicule	Fas.				
Page (cont.)	Pg.				
Issue (No.)	No.	Part	Pt.	Page	Pg.
:	:	:	:	:	:
Lieferung	Lfg.				
Teil	T.	Lieferung	Lfg.	Seite	St.
Teil	T.	Seite	St.	Seite (cont.)	St.
Seite	St.	Seite (cont.)	St.		
Lieferung	Lfg.				
Part	Pt.				
Halft(e)	Hal.				
Seite (cont.)	St.				
Chast	Cha.				
Vypchsk	Vyp.	Chast	Cha.		
Chast	Cha.				

Note: Further term patterns may be defined as needed to cover other languages and term orders.

*Denotes the volume analog for binding purposes and the placement of the bound indicator (/) in a holding statement.

Reprinted from Audrey N. Grosch, "Theory and Design of Serial Holding Statements in Computer-Based Serials Systems," *The Serials Librarian* 1, no. 4: 344-45 (Summer 1977).

should be compatible with the standard. The library which decides to use a compatible holdings notation will require additional programming to integrate their holdings into a serial union list.

Second, should the "natural language identifiers" or "captions" be present in the enumeration of the holdings? The *ANSI Standard for Serial Holdings Statements at the Summary Level* specifies that these captions are to be omitted from the enumeration. This omission will result in summary level holdings like 1:1-3:5, 3:10-3:12, 4:1-. The 1:1-3:5 indicates all volumes are held which fall between series 1, volume 1 and series 3, volume 5 (series 1, volumes 1-25, series 2, volumes 1-25, and series 3, volumes 1-5). The 3:10-3:12 represents series 3, volumes 10, 11, and 12. The 4:1- represents series 4, volume 1 and to continue. Although the ANSI holdings notation is not always clear, omitting the captions does remove the further work of standards for the captions. For example, which is desirable as a caption: volume, vol, v., or vols? The ANSI standard goes on to indicate that if the absence of captions will cause serious confusion, the information may be entered in the local notes data element of the format.[7]

Some systems for serial holdings include the captions in the enumeration and others do not. In Ohio State's LCS and in Northwestern's online systems, the captions are included with the enumeration in the holdings field and in the resulting displays. The University of Illinois version of LCS does not include natural language identifiers in the serial holdings statements. (This system is described in the appendix.) The OCLC serial check-in subsystem provides a separate field for defining the subfields in the holdings field. Thus, in the OCLC system, the user must consult two data fields to secure the holdings for a title.

Third, should the detailed holdings be entered into the holdings file so that summary holdings may be automatically created through character manipulation? Summary holdings statements are desirable for query either in an online system or in printed lists. In those systems in which the holdings file will be used only for query or only for circulation, the automatic derivation of summary holdings is not necessary. The UCLA Biomedical Library Control System for Serials and the University of Minnesota Biomedical Library Serials System are designed to do such manipulation. The Northwestern Library's serial check-in and the Ohio State University Libraries' LCS were designed without this capability.

Fourth, at what point will the check-in and bindery functions interface with the holdings function? In the UCLA and North-western system, check-in, bindery, and holdings are integrated. In both of these systems, the check-in in online, and the holdings notation is merely changed when the volume is bound. The OSU Libraries' current use of LCS does not include check-in, thus the holdings file is updated when a bound volume is added to the collection. The integration of the holdings from check-in forward is important from the standpoint of public service and staff efficiency.

Fifth, will the holdings notation be used to support circulation? If this is planned, then the holdings must identify the physical volumes, the actual physical pieces that will be circulated. Although bar code numbers or any other numbering system can, for example, provide adequate control for circulation, the publisher assigned numbers must be available for staff and patron information. If the public service for serial holdings is not part of the circulation system, then summary holdings notation will probably be sufficient.

Sixth, how will incomplete holdings be included? This can be done either by noting that certain items are not held or by listing only those which are held. In LCS, we are using statements of what is held rather than what is missing.

Seventh, how will the holdings of the same title in different formats — paper, microfilm, machine-readable, braille, etc. — be included in the system? Until the summer of 1980, the OSU Libraries cataloged and classified each format separately, thus listing the holdings in separate records. This practice has now been changed to classify all formats together and to show the format type as part of the volume identifier. The indications are that this is going to be a successful change.

ROUTING CONTROL

Routing of newly received periodical issues is a very simple computer application if the library policy supports the activity. Routing is more often done by special libraries than in public or academic libraries; however, the procedure would be the same regardless of the library. The four steps in any routing system include (1) the creation of a list of the journals to be routed; (2) distributing the list to the individuals eligible for the service; (3) the individuals identify the titles they wish to receive; and (4) the requests are returned to the library.

A routing system in the Arthur D. Little Management Library is reported by Blair in *Special Libraries* in 1972[8] and by Palmer in *Case Studies in Library Computer Systems* in 1973.[9] This system has three files: (1) a file of employee records with name, address, and employee number for each individual receiving the routing service; (2) a file of all journals to be routed and an identification number for the title; and (3) a list of the periodicals to be routed to each employee. This arrangement reduces the effort of updating names, addresses, and choice changes. The computer prints out the routing slips in duplicate so that one copy may accompany the journal, and one copy of the routing slip is also on file in the library until the issue is returned. The program will also produce a listing of all employees, their addresses, employee numbers, and a list of the serials currently routed to them. Once a year these reports are sent for revision to those who use the service.

BINDERY CONTROL

The primary objectives of automated bindery control include:

1. Production of binding slips
2. Identification of volumes ready to bind
3. A record of volumes at the bindery from which the volumes not returned on schedule may be identified.

The computer-assisted bindery control modules are either part of an automated check-in system or are a stand-alone bindery control system. Each bindery system works slightly differently. In all cases, however, binding slips and/or binding lists are produced to accompany the volumes sent to the bindery.

These binding slips and/or lists are created from records which generally contain the following data: title (or author and title), binding color, class of binding, color of lettering, lettering style, lettering size, lettering location (for title, volume, and call number), instructions for handling advertisements, indexes, and title page. The systems examined have most of the binding data coded in fixed-length fields. Some bindery records also contain issue frequency, number of issues bound together, and binding frequency.[10]

The identification of the volumes to be bound can be accomplished automatically using the issue frequency and the number of issues bound together or using the frequency of binding, e.g., once every three months or once each year. The Library Binding Company updates the Baylor University Library bindery file annually at which time the binding slips for the next twelve months are printed.[11] Several bindery control systems allow the production of binding slips (lists) on request. These systems allow the request as part of the serial check-in system.[12]

The third function of a bindery control system is to provide a record of volumes at the bindery. This record should be accessible by call number and title as well as the bindery shipment. Online circulation systems can be used to charge volumes to the bindery[13] and will provide overdue notices when volumes at the bindery are not returned on schedule. An example of an Ohio State University bindery charge on LCS appears in figure 1, which shows V58 (volume 58) charged to RESSPEBQ (Special Materials bindery quota). This LCS record may be accessed by title, author, and call number, but the volume cannot be accessed or otherwise associated with a specific bindery shipment.

```
HN51J8      SOCIAL FORCES     NOLC      291665    1922      3        SER
01      001      MAI
02      002 NOCIR SOC
03      003 NOCIR UND
04 MAI 001      S              CURRENT ISSUES IN PERIODICAL ROOM
05 MAI 001           1979-1980 V58              0 CHGD   RESSPEBQ   800708/800916
06 SPE 001           1979-1980 V58(MICROFILM)
07 MAI 001           1978-1979 V57
08 SPE 001           1978-1979 V57(MICROFILM)
09 MAI 001           1977-1978 V56              0 SNAGD 79070745   800327/800328
PAGE 1 MORE ON NEXT PAGE.  ENTER PD2
```

Figure 1. LCS Library Location Record with Serial Holdings

The UCLC Biomedical Library records volumes which are at the bindery in the serials system, and the volume status may be searched at online terminals.[14] This system also prepares packing lists which list the volumes in the bindery shipment.[15]

CIRCULATION CONTROL

The primary function of a library circulation system is to maintain a record of each book on loan. This record includes the identification of the borrower, the identification of the book, and the date the book is to be returned.

The identification of the book frequently is the shelf location description of call number, copy number, and volume number. The call number and copy number are assigned by the holding library, but the volume number used is often the number assigned by the publisher. The publisher's numbering system for volumes frequently is complex. Many automated circulation systems do not provide a sufficiently flexible data field for the volume so as to permit intelligible volume identification.

The following discussion of circulation control will be based upon a description of the serial holdings in the Library Control System (LCS), a circulation system which is in operation at The Ohio State University (OSU), the State University of New York at Albany, the University of Illinois, and other Illinois libraries participating on LCS through the Illinois Higher Education Cooperative Act (HECA). In addition to serving as a circulation system, LCS is available at most of these libraries to the patrons through public search terminals. The Ohio State University Libraries intend for LCS to be the replacement for the card catalogs.[16] The examples in this discussion are from the OSU Library Control System. The Illinois LCS is described in the appendix.

The Ohio State University Libraries are composed of twenty-six department libraries, two undergraduate libraries, and the Main Library. The libraries' collection contains approximately 3.6 million volumes for 1.6 million titles of which 65,000 are serial titles. The libraries circulate nearly two million items per year. Approximately one third of the holdings and one half of the circulation occur in the locations outside the Main Library. Eighteen of the locations circulate serial volumes, which makes the provision for serial control in the circulation system important. This university library system serves a campus community of more than 70,000 students, faculty, and staff.

In addition, in March 1979, the State Library of Ohio began using the OSU LCS for the circulation control of approximately 150,000 titles. This sharing of LCS has facilitated reciprocal loan of materials to the users of each library.[17]

When the Library Control System began operation in November 1970, no serial holdings were listed for the titles. Although most serial titles were on LCS with copy numbers and locations, no volumes were included (see figure 2). The display of the original LCS serial title record included call number, author if present,

```
HN51J8      SOCIAL FORCES      NOLC    291665    1922    3    SER
01      001          MAI
02      002 NOCIR SOC
03      003 NOCIR UND
PAGE 1 END
```

Figure 2. LCS Library Location Record for Serial Titles (pre-1977)

title, Library of Congress card number, the code SER for serial, date of first issue, and the number of copies, copy numbers, and location codes. The holdings capability of the early LCS included only a three-character volume number, which was found quickly to be insufficient for many serial volumes and thus was not used for any serial volumes.

The specifications for adding volume holdings to LCS were written in 1974-75 following the charge to add serial holdings to LCS to provide for online access to the libraries' serial holdings for patrons and staff and to secure the benefits of automated serial holdings control. This charge was further clarified to specify that the system should provide for the entry of physical volumes to allow the circulation control of serial holdings. The holdings were added, and serial volumes were first circulated in August 1977.[18]

The specifications provide for one holdings record for each physical volume or each summary holdings statement. The fields in each holdings record include copy number, location code, circulation condition code, holding type, unique identification, year of publication, and bibliographic unit. In addition, if a volume is charged out, the circulation data, including borrower ID, date borrowed, and date due, appears on the same line of the library location display. Thus, the patron learns if a volume is available at the same time the patron learns that the library owns the volume desired (see figure 1).

The circulation condition code specifies to the computer the length of time for which a physical volume may circulate. On LCS, the condition code may be from one day to ten weeks, noncirculating, or withdrawn; however, most periodical volumes at OSU have condition codes of one week or less, and several department libraries do not circulate periodicals.

The holdings type allows LCS to have both summary holdings statements and physical volume statements. A holdings line displays an "S" when more than one physical volume is represented in the statement. LCS will not permit the charge of a summary holdings statement regardless of the condition code shown. If no "S" is displayed on the holdings line, the record is for a physical volume, which will circulate according to its circulation condition code.

The years entered in the year field are the first and last year which are applicable to the record. The inclusion of the year field in the record permits the user to retrieve a specific year in a search request. Figure 3 illustrates an LCS search for the 1975 volumes of the periodical *Social Forces*.

```
SEARCH:     DSC/HN51J8,Y=1975

RESPONSE:

HN51J8          SOCIAL FORCES       NOLC      291665   1922        3    SER
01 MAI 001              1975-1976 V54                0 SNAGD 79070745   800327/800328
02 SPE 001              1975-1976 V54(MICROFILM)
03 MAI 001              1974-1975 V53
04 SPE 001              1974-1975 V53(MICROFILM)
05 SOC 002 NOCIR S 1955-1977 V34-55
06 UND 003 NOCIR S 1972-1975 V51-53
07 UND 003 NOCIR   1975      V54N01-2
PAGE 1 END
```

Figure 3. LCS Search for Serial Holdings by Year

The unique identification field in the holdings record is the equivalent of a volume field. We chose not to call it the volume field because many serial publications are not identified by volume but rather by number or year. This field is of variable length with a maximum of 255 characters. The length and content of the field is to agree with the labeling on the volume. The sequence of the information within this field also should correctly represent the numbering scheme assigned by the publisher to the serial pieces. The content of the field has some limitations. Periods are omitted, decimals are not. At OSU, commas are replaced with spaces, and slashes are replaced by hyphens. The slashes and commas could not be used in this field at OSU because they are used in the LCS commands. The Illinois LCS allows these punctuation marks. The natural language identifiers are included in the field. The unique identification in an LCS circulation transaction is equivalent to a volume in other circulation systems.

The bibliographic unit is not displayed, except in maintenance transactions. This data field normally contains the enumeration of the primary level of the unique identification. For example, the unique identification of v.1, pt.2 has a bibliographic unit of 1, and the unique identification of ser. 2, v.34 should have the bibliographic unit of 34. The bibliographic unit is used to sequence the records in the terminal display; it permits the user to locate a volume, the exact labeling of which is not known (see figure 4).

```
SEARCH:     DSC/HN51J8,V=50

RESPONSE:

HN51J8    '   SOCIAL FORCES      NOLC    291665    1922    3    SER
01 MAI 001              1971-1972 V50
02 SPE 001              1971-1972 V50(MICROFILM)
03 SOC 002 NOCIR S 1955-1977 V34-55
04 SOC 002 NOCIR   1922-1972 IND V1-50
PAGE 1 END
```

Figure 4. LCS Serial Holdings Search by Volume

Recently, the OSU Libraries implemented a policy of purchasing microform in lieu of binding the volumes of some serial titles. The procedure for implementing this policy is to assign to the microform reproduction the classification and copy number of the printed copy and to indicate the type of reproduction in the unique identification following the publisher assigned numbers, for example, V58(MICROFICHE). This policy is to be applied retrospectively to previous purchases of serial titles in microform.

The online maintenance of the LCS holdings records has been programmed so that there are three levels of authorization: (1) not permitted; (2) single location; or (3) all locations. The terminals which may maintain all LCS holdings records are located in the central Technical Services. Approximately, fifteen library locations have been authorized to maintain the holdings housed in the specific location. This capability to do decentralized online maintenance may at some future time allow decentralized serial check-in. The decentralized maintenance is not fully used at this time.

Currently, serial holdings are added to LCS at different times depending on the type of serial. The serials which arrive bound, ready to circulate or which will not be bound are added to LCS by the central Technical Services after the pieces have been checked in on the central manual file. Periodicals, which are received as issues and which will be bound when complete, are entered into LCS when they are sent to the bindery. Those locations which are authorized to do maintenance add the volume to the LCS Holdings File before sending the volume to the bindery and then charge the volume to the bindery. Those locations which are not authorized to do online maintenance charge the volume on LCS to the bindery using an older, less intelligible entry. When these latter volumes are returned from the bindery, the central Technical Services enter the newly bound volumes into the Holdings File from the bindery record.

LCS serves as a holding record for serial holdings which are bound and ready to circulate. However, both patrons and library staff need to know the holdings of current periodical issues as well. This need could be satisfied by LCS if the check-in function were added, and the checked-in holdings made available at the public terminals. Because check-in has not been functionally described for the programmers, the decision has been made to add notes to the holdings records. Figure 1 includes an example of a note.

The policy and procedures for using the LCS Holdings File are still in development at the Ohio State University Libraries. As the procedures are developed, other desirable capabilities for the system are also identified for future programming.

CONCLUSION

No current serial holdings system has completely integrated all functions of serials holdings inventory and control. Several systems — UCLA Biomedical Library, University of Minnesota Biomedical Library, and Northwestern — have successfully, although not consistently, recorded summary holdings statements; but summary holdings statements are not compatible with routing, binding, and circulation control. The Library Control System at Ohio State and Illinois has provided for the identification of individual volumes for circulation control but does not include current issues in the holdings.

Serials control systems for individual libraries need to accommodate the identification of holdings at the physical piece level allowing the identification of these pieces with the natural language identifier. Ideally, the serials system should create summary holdings statements from the physical piece level and allow access to either physical piece records or summary statements.

Last, the development of the ANSI standards for serial publication patterns and detailed serial holdings statements should be monitored closely. Once these standards are published, new serial systems should incorporate the standards in the record format and terminal display.

REFERENCES

1. Audrey N. Grosch, "Theory and Design of Serial Holdings Statements in Computer-Based Serial Systems," *The Serials Librarian* (Summer 1977): 341-52.

2. *American National Standard for Serial Holdings Statements at the Summary Level* (New York: American National Standards Institute, Inc., 1980), p. 3.

3. Ibid., p. 13.

4. James Rush to Ann Ekstrom, 11 June 1979. Gerald Lowell has since been appointed chairman of the ANSI Z39 Subcommittee on Serial Publication Pattern Codes.

5. American National Standard Institute Z39 Program Committee, "Charge to ANSI Subcommittee E," April 1980.

6. International Federation of Library Associations and Institutions, "UNESCO/IFLA Union List Project," December 1979.

7. *American National Standard for Serial Holdings Statements at the Summary Level,* p. 14.

8. Joan Blair, "Routing Slips from the Computer," *Special Libraries* 63 (Feb. 1972): 82-84.

9. Richard P. Palmer, *Case Studies in Library Computer Systems* (New York: Bowker, 1973), pp. 101-6.

10. Linda F. Crismond and Sylvia B. Fatzer, "Automated Serials Check-in and Binding Procedures at the San Francisco Public Library," *Proceedings of the 32nd Annual Meeting of the American Society for Information Science* (Westport, Conn.: Greenwood Publishing, 1969), pp. 13-20; Iris P. Jeffress, "Data-Bind Computerized Binding Slips," *The Library Scene* 4 (Dec. 1975): 22-24; Sandra Dennis to Susan Miller, 20 Aug. 1980.

11. Jeffress, p. 22.

12. Northwestern University Library and Inforonics are examples.

13. William J. Willmering, "On-Line Centralized Serials Control," *The Serials Librarian* 1 (Spring 1977): 243-49.

14. James Fayollat, "On-Line Serials Control System in a Large Biomedical Library: 1) Description of the System," *Journal of the American Society for Information Science* 23 (Sept.-Oct. 1972): 320.

15. James Fayollat, "On-Line Serials Control System in a Large Biomedical Library Part III: Comparison of On-Line and Batch Operations and Cost Analysis," *Journal of the American Society for Information Science* 24 (March-April 1973): 84.

16. Susan L. Miller, "The Evolution of an On-Line Catalog," in *New Horizons for Academic Libraries,* edited by Robert D. Stueart and Richard D. Johnson (New York: K. G. Saur, 1979), pp. 193-204; Susan L. Miller, "The Changing Role of A Circulation System: The OSU Experience," *RQ* 20 (Fall 1980): 47-52.

17. A. Robert Thorson and Phyllis B. Davis, "Borrowing Made Easy: Automated Resource Sharing in Ohio," *Wilson Library Bulletin* 53 (April 1980): 502-04.

18. Carol R. Krumm, "Conversion of Serial Holdings to On-Line Automated Library Control System at The Ohio State University Libraries," accepted for publication in *The Serial Librarian.*

Serials Control by Agents

BETSY L. HUMPHREYS

People who have worked at serials acquisition, check-in, claiming, payment posting, or binding will not be surprised to learn that there is no such thing as complete serials control by agents. We have not yet attained the ideal state in which the library manager can drive all serials staff into the reference room and simply buy out of all the hassles and frustrations of serials control. Even given the determination and money to launch such a program, it is still necessary to have someone in-house making sure that the Brazilian *Revista de Medicina* is not supplied in place of the Argentinian one, that the *New Yorker* is actually renewed for next year, that the first January issue of *Biological Abstracts* arrives before April, and that the latest title change of the *Journal of Nuclear Medicine* is recorded.

But once it is acknowledged that complete serials control by anyone is rare, it should be obvious that there are a variety of existing, developing, and possible serials processing services to be provided by commercial serials agents which can be of real assistance to libraries. All of these services cost something, although in some cases not more than what is already being paid to obtain basic subscription handling, and the value of any specific service will vary from library to library.

The National Library of Medicine (NLM) was a pioneer in the use of subscription agents for many serials control functions and

Betsy L. Humphreys is chief of the Technical Services Division of the National Library of Medicine.

has enjoyed the direct and indirect benefits of an off-site dealer check-in program for several years. While it is certainly true that NLM has an unusual set of staffing problems, a relatively large budget, a large computing facility, and unique service requirements, it does not follow that serials processing services provided by subscription agents are not useful for libraries with very different circumstances. Other libraries may seek such services out of different motives, and the services best suited to their needs may differ from those used by NLM, but they can still receive real assistance in serials processing from subscription agents.

Serials subscription agents can provide a solution to two basic library problems: lack of manpower to process serials and lack of systems support and other resources needed to automate serials control. For NLM, which is subject to federal personnel ceilings and hiring freezes and has limited access to student and volunteer help, the need to augment its existing serials staff was the prime motivating force for the development of the dealer check-in program. Although inadequate staffing is becoming a universal problem, for many libraries a desire to take advantage of subscription agents' automated serials databases and software capabilities may be a stronger motive for pursuing services beyond regular subscription handling.

SOME ALTERNATIVES

Of course, use of subscription agents for serials processing is not the only solution to the problems of acquiring adequate serials staffing and developing automated serials control. It may be useful to review briefly some of the alternatives to provide a context for assessing services available from subscription agents.

In augmenting scarce serials staff, one option is the employment of contract labor for ongoing serials functions. Many libraries use the contract mechanism very infrequently, if at all, and are inclined to think of it in terms of large special projects, such as the conversion of retrospective catalog records to machine-readable form or the implementation of a circulation system. Still, the most typical library contract is for an ongoing serials function, the binding of paperbound serial issues. Where they exist, such contracts often began as an alternative to labor intensive in-house binding. Individual libraries can easily lose sight of this fact because binding contracts are often handled at the county, city, or university level to achieve economy of scale.

To alleviate its staffing problems, NLM has for several years performed its entire bindery preparation function under contract, and in July of 1980 the preparation of serials for micro-preservation was incorporated into the same agreement. Since NLM binds 32,000 volumes and microfilms as many as 1,000,000 pages annually, use of a contractor for preparing and reshelving materials releases several NLM staff members for public service functions and other processing activities which are less amenable to contract support. Under NLM's preparation contract, the contractor maintains a small staff on site at NLM to pull materials from the stacks and has additional staff on their own premises for final preparation and shipment of materials to another contractor for actual binding. Returned bound volumes are received and checked by the off-site contract staff and then reshelved by the contract employees working on site at NLM.

The entire bindery preparation operation is controlled by the binding module of NLM's automated Master Serials System in combination with data in the bibliographic module. The system maintains the record of what has been pulled, prepared, and sent to the binder and is used to generate shelf changes for units to be pulled, instructions to the binder, summary statistics, and other processing products. The preparation contractor is able to search all relevant modules of the NLM serials system and has complete responsibility for online and batch maintenance of the binding module. Similar procedures are followed for microfilming preparation, using the micropreservation module of the serials system.

Successful use of a contractor for ongoing serials processing functions requires a high and predictable volume of transactions of a particular type, a well-written statement of work, a rigorous contractor selection process, ongoing monitoring of contract performance, and, of course, the money to pay the contractor. Given these conditions, contract labor could be used for check-in and claiming as well as bindery preparation. The volume requirements could be met by a system or universitywide contract or even a multi-system contract if an individual library's transaction level is insufficient to justify contract action. The money is obviously a more serious problem. However, if a library or group of libraries is currently using full-time paid employees to perform a particular function, it may be worthwhile to compare the annual cost of that labor (including benefits, any predictable salary increases, and the associated overhead) with the probable cost of contracting out the function. As federal government agencies and local jurisdictions are forced to reduce the size of the public payroll, the contract alternative may become more attractive.

Contractual arrangements are less likely to be used to obtain ongoing automated serials control, although they might be used for the development of special purpose software. For most libraries, however, in-house development of serials control software is the least attractive approach to serials automation.

Of the available or projected alternatives to automated serials control by subscription agents, one of the most obvious is use of serials control features available from general purpose utilities or special networks. Unfortunately, the immediate prospect for full serials control using any of the major utilities is not bright. Full serials services are available from PHILSOM, but this network serves biomedical libraries only. Other alternatives are to use commercially produced serials automation software either by purchasing it for use on local hardware or by paying for its use on the vendor's hardware, or to use serials software developed by other libraries. In both cases, the serials software may be part of a system performing multiple library functions. Unfortunately, the range and sophistication of serials control features in many general library packages or even in special serials software may not meet all of a library's basic serials control needs, and the availability of hardware and systems support staff may be a problem.

Yet another option, which has been used by NLM for the past five years, is the application of a general purpose, commercially available database management system (DBMS) to serials control functions. NLM has had great success building and maintaining a Master Serials System[1] consisting of eight modules, using a DBMS software called INQUIRE, which is a proprietary product of Infodata Systems, Inc. This same software, which has an extremely powerful user syntax for searching, maintenance, and flexible report generation, is also used by NLM for control of monograph acquisitions, for the production of bills for users of MEDLINE and other NLM online retrieval files, and for management of the NLM grant program, to mention only a few of its applications at the library. NLM also assisted the White House Conference on Library and Information Services by creating and storing INQUIRE files, including the text of all resolutions passed at the state conferences preceding the White House Conference. This database was used extensively by delegates to the national conference.

As was pointed out in a recent communication to the *Journal of*

Library Automation,[2] many libraries would do well to investigate the DBMS possibilities. In cases where the library's parent institution has a computing facility, a useful DBMS package may already be installed for some general administrative functions. Many computer service bureaus and time-sharing networks also provide access to various DBMS softwares, which could solve some of the hardware and support staff problems.

These alternatives to serials processing services by subscription agents are mentioned not to confuse the issue, but to provide a context in which to evaluate services by agents. A library has several serials automation options today and will have a much improved choice of avenues in a few years. (Although that statement may be another example of what Samuel Johnson called "the triumph of hope over experience.") For many libraries none of the options now available is such a bargain in terms of their present software, hardware, personnel, and budget and so well suited to their operational needs that they can afford to ignore special services provided by serials subscription agents as a possible method for handling some of their serials control functions.

RANGE OF SERVICES PROVIDED

In approaching any service available from dealers, some librarians fear (sometimes with good cause) that subscription agents may attempt to overcharge their customers and gradually inflate agreed-upon service charges. To deny that this can and does occur would be ridiculous, but it is not the norm. It is also true that the opportunity for pursuing such practices undetected increases as larger service charges are paid for special services. The chance of this occurring should not prevent any library from investigating and using subscription agents for serials services if such an arrangement seems beneficial. Librarians obviously have an obligation to monitor any such arrangement to make sure they are paying a fair price for a good service, and they have the option of discontinuing business with any agent if they determine that this is not the case. A variety of agents provide special serials handling services, so librarians can shop around for the features and prices which best suit their individual needs. Taking time to understand an agent's invoicing procedures will avoid later problems. There are significant differences in the traditional practices of United States and European agents.

61

Although there are still some unautomated subscription agents, most of the services described here presuppose that the agent has automated the bibliographic, customer, publisher, and invoice data required to control subscriptions and, in many cases, has augmented the bibliographic and customer data to support additional services. Indeed, many of these services cannot be offered economically (or at all) unless the agent has an extensive automated system. However, some future possibilities, involving direct interaction between a subscription agent's staff and a library's own automated system, would not require the agent to have extensive automation.

There are five general categories of services provided by subscription agents which can contribute to the ongoing control of serials by libraries. These are: (1) subscription handling; (2) dissemination of bibliographic information related to serials; (3) assistance in library fiscal control and budget allocation and projection; (4) services related to actual issue handling and check-in; and (5) support for union lists. The service package best suited to the needs of any individual library is likely to contain a combination of features from more than one of these categories. This paper does not provide an exhaustive explanation of all available services, but attempts to describe the range of services offered and some of the advantages and disadvantages associated with them.

SUBSCRIPTION HANDLING

To begin with the most familiar, subscription handling is the primary service offered by subscription agents. This basic service includes contacting publishers to determine rates, placing orders for libraries with accompanying prepayment as necessary, presenting customer libraries with consolidated invoices for serials ordered, and renewing subscriptions either automatically or based on annual renewal instructions from their customers. Basic subscription handling also includes claiming with the publisher (and providing proof of payment for) any specific issues or whole subscriptions reported as not received by customer libraries. At the moment, most libraries send their orders to agents through the mail and receive confirmation or other information from agents by the same means. Some agents will offer online transmission of orders and communication on existing orders in the near future.

Although subscription agents used to receive discounts from

most publishers and pass some savings on to their customers, publishers' discounts to dealers are much less prevalent now, particularly among American publishers, and the average service charge for basic subscription handling is between 4 and 10 percent of the purchase price of all serials handled for a library by an agent. Some dealers have a maximum charge per individual title, which prevents a customer from paying exorbitant handling charges for very expensive individual titles such as *Chemical Abstracts*. In some cases, the service charge can be offset by additional credit offered by agents to customers who prepay a major portion of their account. Also, some of the other services which will be described are offered at no additional charge and will increase the value of the basic subscription handling service for some libraries. While it is true that there are still some agents willing to offer across-the-board discounts on subscription prices, their ability to provide good service consistently is questionable.

If the discount incentive is eliminated, the major advantages of using a basic subscription handling service are savings in staff work hours needed for ordering and invoice processing and, in many cases, more rapid payment to the publishers. Libraries with a small number of serials and the ability to dispatch a check quickly may operate relatively efficiently without a subscription agent, although such libraries often do not have the necessary tools and resources to determine current publisher address and price information. Once a library is dealing in the hundreds or thousands of serials, use of subscription agents leads to a real savings in time spent verifying prices and addresses, renewing subscriptions, and and processing invoices, as well as in postage costs. Unfortunately, there is no small group of publishers which account for the majority of serials. For example, the approximately 2,600 serials covered by *Index Medicus* are produced by over 1,000 different publishers. Dealing even with that many annual mailings and invoices is an extremely expensive proposition.

Many libraries are part of larger institutions with involved payment structures. Because of lengthy payment procedures, it may take several weeks or months to issue checks to publishers. For many subscription items which require prepayment, these delays can seriously affect the start up of new subscriptions and cause breaks in the receipt of established ones.

It is paradoxical that some librarians perceive the disadvantages of basic subscription handling by agents to be the exact reverse of the two advantages just described (that is, they believe that the service is more expensive than handling subscriptions directly and that there are greater delays, particularly in the start up of new subscriptions, if the agent's service is used). The perception that the subscription agent is more expensive may be simply a function of the fact that the payment of the agent's service charge is a much more visible expense than the cost of the staff hours involved in ordering, renewing, and processing serials invoices and the cost of the postage involved in these transactions with many different publishers. The value received for a subscription agent's services is, in large part, dependent on the cost of the library's serials labor force, and, in the end, each library must assess the cost situation for itself. For many large libraries, a $50,000 service charge paid for handling $1 million worth of serials would not come close to buying enough in-house staff to handle subscriptions as expeditiously and successfully as can be done by subscription agents, even if the funds could be diverted to personnel.

In some specific cases, particularly with monographic series for which publishers are willing to send the volume with an accompanying invoice, it is quicker to go direct, but overall, given the prepayment problems discussed earlier, use of an agent will probably be faster. Agents maintain extensive files of title, address, and price information and in many cases can dispatch a check and an order immediately without a preliminary inquiry to the publisher. Lapsed subscriptions due to late payment are much less likely to occur when an agent is used.

BIBLIOGRAPHIC INFORMATION RELATED TO SERIALS

The second category of services supplied by agents, which involves the dissemination of bibliographic information on serials, began as a byproduct of basic subscription handling and is usually offered to regular customers without cost. Much of the data required for services in this category are captured by the subscription agent as part of the subscription handling activity and, with additional programming, can be output in various products useful to libraries.

One of the most familiar services in this category is the announcement of new titles, title changes, cessations, suspensions, etc., which is derived from the bibliographic information which the dealer maintains in support of subscription handling. This information can be extremely valuable as a selection tool and as an aid in keeping existing library records up to date. Its value is necessarily dependent on the completeness and accuracy of the bibliographic data the dealer maintains and is willing to display.

The quality of bibliographic data provided varies considerably from agent to agent. Some subscription agents have been very interested in using standard identifiers (e.g., ISSN, OCLC numbers), obtaining information from authoritative sources to add to their files (at least two agents have incorporated data from NLM's SERLINE file in their systems), and maintaining such special data as coverage by abstracting and indexing services, various subject headings and class numbers, and actual descriptions of the content of publications. Most agents include all the pertinent data they have available in their title announcement bulletins, although a few still give insufficient publication information (e.g., no city or country) to allow a library to place either a direct order or one with another agent.

In the past, it was common for agents to issue consolidated bulletins of new title and publication change information, which forced some librarians to wade through many announcements of no relevance to their collections in order to reach the few pertinent ones. Some agents have addressed this problem by dividing their new title announcements into subject groupings and by providing customized lists of changes, suspensions, cessations, etc., which deal only with the titles a particular customer has on order. Agents also provide customized lists of all titles handled for a library which may be used by reference staff and patrons in some libraries.

In an effort to improve customer access to a range of bibliographic data for serials, some subscription agents will offer customers online access to the agents' files of bibliographic, publisher, and price information. Some also plan to mount the authoritative records contained on MARC-S tapes and in the CONSER database on their own systems and make these available online to their customers. Although there are no immediate plans to use CONSER records as the bibliographic basis for subscription agent services, this remains a future possibility. Since the provision of online access to bibliographic data by subscription agents is still in the development stage, pricing structures have not been fixed.

FISCAL CONTROL

The third category of services provided by subscription agents, assistance in library fiscal control and budget allocation and projection, also began as a byproduct of regular subscription handling. For several years, some agents have provided summary reports of customer expenditures, as well as renewal lists, by shipping address, by fund account or budget code, by subject parameters, by cost of single items, etc. The amount of customer data (e.g., fund accounts, department indicators, special subject headings) stored by agents varies and therefore so do the expenditure reports and special renewal lists they can generate. Some subscription agents can also provide data on year to year percentage increases in prices over a customer's total list of titles or any of the subsets mentioned above. Faxon has for some years published similar information for all titles in the Faxon database, as well as for different subject areas as indicated by abstracting and indexing service coverage.[3] These services can be extremely helpful in budgeting, in explaining the current state of serials acquisition to top management and various constituent groups, and in assisting difficult selection and cancellation decisions. They provide easy access to data which unautomated libraries can only approximate even after long hours of manual work.

Many agents also offer invoices in machine-readable form to customers who wish to implement automated payment posting on their own systems. Invoices are currently available on cards and on tape and, under the right circumstances, probably could be transferred to a customer's computer directly by a remote job entry device or similar mechanism. Although nothing comparable is offered today, online input of invoice data to a customer library's system by a subscription agent is not beyond the realm of possibility either. Also, there is no technical reason why agents cannot eventually supply machine-readable data to utilities used by their customers as well as to an individual library's system, but the necessary work on the utilities' end is probably at least a few years off.

Machine-assisted review and processing of invoices is one area which promises significant labor savings to any library with a large serials collection and access to automation support. In the course of a year, a serials staff dealing with a collection of 20,000 titles might easily review 30,000 line items on invoices (including credits and added charges) in order to find fewer than 10 percent of them in error. Yet the responsibility to verify that correct amounts are being spent for needed materials remains. Machine processing could assist in the rapid identification of this 10 percent. NLM has planned for the machine processing of invoices for several years and is currently receiving machine-readable invoices from some dealers. The project should become operational in 1981. According to dealers who offer this service, there are relatively few libraries actually using it at present.

ISSUE HANDLING AND CHECK-IN

The fourth category of services provided by subscription agents involves support of actual issue handling and check-in. This category splits logically into two groups: issue handling services in which the agent actually receives and processes materials for its client and services involving the client's use of the dealer's automated system and software to support check-in performed by the client's staff. The first group of services has been available, although on a somewhat restricted basis, for several years. The second group, inspired by agents' involvement with the first, is in an experimental phase, but should have wider availability in the next two years.

The most widespread form of actual issue handling by subscription agents involves the collection of issues for reshipping in bulk, usually to overseas customers. In this service, the agent places orders for titles to be mailed to the agent's address and then packages groups of them for shipment, typically by some air freight mechanism, to various library customers. The agent does not actually process the issues (i.e., call numbers, shelving locations, property stamps, or routing slips are not attached to them), but will send some claims for unreceived items. The main advantage of this service is that it avoids the delay of sea mail as well as the costs of individual issue air mail for foreign publications. (A similar service, minus claiming, can also be arranged directly with an air freight company. For a few years, NLM had all European *Index Medicus* titles mailed to Emory Air Freight in Frankfurt, Germany, for weekly shipment to the library.) The cost of this service includes shipping charges, but is otherwise not significantly greater than the price of regular subscription handling.

Full check-in of issues by dealers is a more recent service begun in response to a demand voiced by the National Library of Medicine. The original idea came in 1971 from Salvatore Costabile, then deputy chief of the Technical Services Division at NLM and now head of Costabile Associates, a library consultant firm. Dr. Joseph Leiter, associate director for Library Operations, and William Plank, then head of the Serial Records Section at NLM, were instrumental in persuading Swets and Zeitlinger to try the service beginning in 1973. Several other agents were approached at the same time and were skeptical about attempting such a service, but continued requests by NLM throughout the seventies have led to the present situation in which three domestic and four foreign dealers offer full off-site check-in services to NLM. Some of the agents offer similar services to several other customers. The dealers currently involved in the program are EBSCO, Faxon, Harrassowitz, Nijhoff, Readmore, Stevens and Brown, and Swets and Zeitlinger.

As stated before, NLM's main motive for pursuing dealer check-in was a severe labor shortage. When the service began in 1973, none of NLM's internal serials operation was automated. The processing instructions sent to agents included copies of manual serial record cards. Today, most serials functions, including subscription control, missing back issue orders, binding, micropreservation, and authority control for the NLM indexing operation, are automated. Automated data supplied by dealers in the off-site check-in operation are merged into NLM's internal automated system, and a monthly printout from the NLM system supplies updated processing instructions to agents participating in the program. NLM also manages an automated national biomedical holdings project which will eventually be used for union list generation and automated routing of interlibrary loan requests. Several publications and the SERLINE retrieval file are generated from NLM's serials system. Although NLM's serials automation picture has changed dramatically in the last eight years, the value of off-site check-in to the library as a substitute for scarce labor remains. The existence of the program, in combination with the unique requirements of the extremely large volume of serial document requests received by the library, has definitely influenced NLM's decision to assign a relatively low priority to the development or acquisition of an online check-in system for the library's use.

To outline the off-site check-in service briefly, the agents notify publishers to mail the client's subscriptions to the agents' premises. When issues are received by the agents, they check them in (i.e., they create a description of the issue received), claim skipped issues as necessary, and process the issues according to instructions provided by the client library. In NLM's case, these processing instructions can include call numbers, property stamps, special shelving and routing locations, indexing instructions, and instructions for bindery preparation staff (e.g., issue completes a volume). The agents attach special notes to new titles, title changes, and any problem items (e.g., extra materials received as a result of a subscription). Issues are batched and shipped to clients once or twice weekly accompanied by an alphabetic packing list describing each issue in the shipment. Another copy of the packing list is mailed separately as a shipment notification. Each month the dealers supply multiple copies of a cumulative alphabetic listing of all issues supplied and claimed for the year to date (i.e., each month's list fully supersedes all previous lists for the same year). These listings are used by serials and reference staff as the record of current serials received by the library. In NLM's case, most agents also send a magnetic tape including data on each issue supplied in the previous month in a format NLM has specified. Since NLM requires automated data, several dealers have developed or are developing their own online check-in systems to support the program.

On the library's end, using NLM's procedures as an example, a team of two serials staff members compare items in each shipment to the packing list and to a printout produced from NLM's system which includes bibliographic data and processing instructions for all titles handled by a particular dealer. Correct items are sent directly to the shelving or routing locations marked on the issues or indicated on the attached routing slips. Any missing items or errors caused by misinterpretation or oversight on the agent's part are reported to that agent when a copy of the packing list is returned acknowledging receipt of the shipment. NLM has all serial invoices (including those for standing order items) mailed separately to the library, so there is no invoice processing during the check-in operation, either by the dealer or library staff.

NLM is currently merging the automated data received from four dealers and hopes to expand this program to all seven dealers in 1981. Progress has been slow on NLM's end due to severe staff shortages, and there is a backlog of tapes to process. It is anticipated that this backlog can be eliminated and that appropriate display formats for the merged check-in data will be developed in 1981. A link to NLM's binding routines is planned which will delete individual issue entries when the issues are incorporated into bound volumes.

The service NLM receives, including regular subscription handling and some of the bibliographic and fiscal control services mentioned, typically costs about 20 percent of the purchase price of all titles handled by the agent plus shipping charges (which can be high, particularly for foreign materials). Agents refigure this charge annually, usually based on the number of individual issues they expect to process, and negotiate it with NLM staff. It may include the cost of processing some free titles. Depending on a variety of factors, increased volume may lead to a decrease in the service charge. The cost of this service may be seen as the most significant disadvantage by some libraries. Again, the cost and availability of in-house labor must be the real deciding factor for any library. NLM's studies of the relative times necessary to process directly received items and off-site check-in shipments show that processing dealer check-in items takes less than half the staff time and about one quarter the elapsed time since it lends itself to a team approach. There are concomitant savings in time needed for mail sorting, in the professional time needed to solve problems associated with the receipt of items not already represented in the NLM file of serial titles, and of course, in the time required for claiming. One interesting benefit is a decrease in time spent processing junk mail.

In comparing its own situation to NLM's, almost any library will find that its issue processing procedures are less complex and time-consuming. This means that, for other libraries, use of a dealer is likely to save less time in the initial processing as well as to require less time in checking shipments. The overall effect may in fact be the same, but any library considering the program must study its own requirements carefully. If a library prefers to receive invoices for standing order items along with the pieces, dealer processing steps must be designed to take this into account.

It has been NLM's experience that, overall, subscription agents process serials accurately. The bibliographic sense of the individuals involved varies from firm to firm, and changes in staffing can lead to a rash of errors, but in general error rates are quite acceptable. Not surprisingly, errors made by subscription agents processing serials are very similar to ones made by any library serials staff — for example, overlooking slight title changes or misreading routing instructions. Language expertise available to foreign agents probably reduces errors (such as failure to identify a particular issue as a special analyzable supplement) in processing foreign publications.

Many of the minor annoyances associated with the program stem from differences in bibliographic entries used by agents and those in NLM's system, in which all entries are straight title. Many agents have used corporate entries in a quite reasonable effort to conform to Library of Congress cataloging. This problem will diminish for NLM in the near future, because several dealers intend to adopt the principles of the *Anglo-American Cataloging Rules,* second edition (*AACR2*). *AACR2* calls for entry under title for many serials which received corporate entry under *AACR1*. If products received from a dealer can replace all or even most of the library's records of its own serials, then discrepancies in entries present little difficulty. Unfortunately, this is unlikely to be the case for many libraries. Although the use of several dealers rather than one is the best approach for NLM for a variety of reasons, it leads to a need to merge dealer-supplied data on the NLM system, and it also complicates that process by introducing multiple formats and increasing the number of batches of data to be processed. These problems would not apply to users of a single vendor.

A generally perceived disadvantage of actual check-in by agents is that it delays receipt of items by the library and also the availability of a unified record indicating what has been received. At present, this is true, and libraries considering this service must weigh this fact against their service requirements. If an air freight arrangement is used for foreign publications, receipt delays may be insignificant for these materials. Depending on the proximity of a domestic agent to the library, the delay for American publications will probably be at least three to five working days. It could be a great deal more, if, for example, UCLA ordered a California state publication to be checked in by an agent in New York. Under certain circumstances, intolerable delays can be easily predicted and the titles involved can be ordered for direct shipment to the library. What the "tolerable" delay is depends on how long the issue is likely to sit before processing once the library receives it and on the size of the demand for the most current issues. Some libraries may believe that the delay is too great for all domestic issues, although that would be an extreme view.

Delay in the availability of a unified record of what has been received is not a major concern to NLM because it is a closed stack library and NLM staff always consult the shelf first to determine what is available for photocopy or on-site use. If the dealer service is going well, very few inquiries are directed to the records. Although NLM is planning for simultaneous receipt and processing of the shipment and its corresponding machine-readable data, it is not an urgent priority.

The service requirements of most other libraries are very different and probably dictate more immediate availability of cumulated receipt information. Possible answers include more frequently updated lists, more frequent dispatch of batches of automated data, online entry of issue data into the library's automated system by the agent (the Universal Serials and Book Exchange performs a service similar to this for NLM, but only in relation to back issues), and online access by the library to the dealer's online check-in system which has been used on its behalf. If multiple agents are used, more frequent addition of agent check-in data to the library's own system (either online by the agent or in batches) may be the only solution to this problem. Even if a single agent is involved, some mechanism must be found for merging data for serials received from other sources (e.g., on exchange) with the agent supplied data. One possibility would be for the library to check-in these few items online into the agent's system, while the agent continues to process the bulk of issues received by the library.

Another possible refinement of the service, particularly for foreign materials, would be for the dealer to provide full or preliminary cataloging of new titles supplied or at least transliteration and translation for their key bibliographic elements. Some of the major foreign subscription agents are also book dealers and have provided similar services to their book customers.

In contrast to the issue handling services, the other approach leaves all receipt processing in the library but provides support to it from the agent's data, software, and hardware. Inclusion of some of the customer's data in the agent's database is a long-standing practice and is necessary for provision of basic subscription handling and certainly for some of the more advanced bibliographic and budgeting assistance products described before. Probably one of the earliest aids to check-in for libraries was the inclusion of special processing codes or addresses on mailing labels (e.g., OCLC numbers). Dealers stored special data as a service to a single customer or group of customers and included these data in the "ship to" address provided to the publisher.

Much more sophisticated services, including online check-in of serials using the vendor's software and storage of check-in data on the vendor's system for online searching by customer libraries, are being developed by some agents. These agents first approached the development of an online check-in system as the most economical means of meeting requirements for the off-site check-in program, and the prototypes of systems which will be offered to other libraries were in some cases developed for the agent's own use in the NLM program.

From preliminary descriptions, some of the online check-in systems being developed by agents appear to address at least two of the potential problems associated with such an approach. They will allow the library to check-in titles not ordered through the agent whose system is being used, and they will permit the library to enter special search keys and alternate title forms if the library's entry for a title is very different from the one used by the agent. There will still be significant advantages in terms of minimal online input of bibliographic data and usability of the dealer's products if the library checks-in on the system of an agent who handles the majority of its subscriptions and uses compatible entries. Since agents' databases include so many serials already, they have similar advantages to large utilities in the area of record creation. Because descriptions of the features of some agents' online check-in systems appear elsewhere in this volume, this paper only addresses some of the general pros and cons of using such a service.

Obviously, the strongest advantages or disadvantages, as the case may be, will be the technical merits and the costs of the system being considered. Its range of features, ease of use, and the likelihood of future augmentation and improvement must all be assessed. Given an acceptable range of features offered at a reasonable cost, the main question becomes how well the service fits in with the library's overall plans for automation.

For many libraries, the eventual goal is probably an "integrated system" — one offered by a utility, a regional network, an in-house system (bought or developed), or a combination of the three. Depending on the current automation support available in-house to a library and the relative progress of its utility toward adequate serials control features, use of an agent's software and hardware may offer a reasonable interim step which can provide the benefits of automated serials control more immediately and may even develop into part of the eventual integrated system. For libraries with existing serials automation, machine-readable invoices and issue handling services like those used by NLM may be more attractive than online use of the vendor's system. For a library with no automation support, use of the dealer's software and hardware may be ideal because it requires no in-house computer support staff.

UNION LISTS

The last category of service provided by subscription agents described here is production of union lists. At least one vendor is offering such a service, which at present essentially involves an indication of which libraries (in a group of institutions specified by the customers) own which titles. The inclusion of actual holdings statements is a planned improvement. This service is available to libraries who do not use the agent at all for subscription handling as well as to regular customers. Regular customers may indicate that they hold titles not ordered through the agent providing the service. At present, the batch input of library symbols is done by the agent.

Union list service should be especially attractive to smaller libraries with no automation support and minimal bibliographic resources. Since the vast majority of bibliographic information needed for union lists is already in the agent's database, the service can be made available at reasonable cost, especially to regular subscription customers. Even without actual holdings statements, union lists produced by dealers may be a real help to libraries which have no reasonably priced alternative.

GENERAL CONSIDERATIONS IN SELECTING
SERVICES

In reviewing any or all of the categories of services described above, there are certain general considerations a library must keep in mind. Some of these have come out in the discussion of the pros and cons of particular services, but deserve restatement. The first concern is a variation on that eternal question: "What is a serial?" In the context of services provided by subscription agents, the important question is, "What does the agent think a serial is?" or, phrased differently, "What range of serials does the agent handle?" In dealing with many European agents, this is a moot point because they handle books, serials, and any strange hybrids of the two. However, in the United States, many subscription agents concentrate on periodicals, and their databases and established publisher connections reflect this. Many American agents also do not handle back issues routinely, while back issue service is part of the standard package offered by many overseas firms. In most cases, American agents are willing to handle monographic series, books-in-part, government documents, and retrospective orders, but their expertise in doing so varies. Any library interested in an agent's services for these groups of serials should look over the list of titles presently handled by the agent and see how many of its own titles are already represented there. The fewer new bibliographic records an agent has to create for a library, the better its service to that library is likely to be.

The second consideration, inevitably mentioned before in connection with various categories of dealer services, is the quality of the bibliographic data in the agent's file. This includes the choice and form of main entry (there may be many list products associated with serials services), the completeness of data available, and the customer's ability to report mistakes and have them corrected. The problems associated with serials entries are numerous and so well known that they need not be reiterated here, but a library should understand what set of rules (if any) the agent is applying and what authoritative sources (if any) are being used. If a library intends to merge fiscal and issue data from one or many agents with its own bibliographic data, varying dealer entries can cause processing headaches, but no long-term problems in tools produced for staff and patron use. If the dealer's data, software, and hardware are used directly, public service products will have the dealer's entry for good or ill. Again, any library contemplating special dealer services should take a good look at entries for a variety of titles already handled by the agent.

The third consideration is whether use of one agent is preferable to use of several. If we discount political constraints which may dictate the division of business among multiple agents, use of a single agent is better in principle for several of the special services described. Budget analysis support and online check-in using a vendor's database and software are two examples of services which will benefit by the concentration of all purchased titles with a single vendor. It is in the area of basic subscription handling, particularly for large serials collections with great depth in certain subject areas, that the special expertise of different agents (e.g., in particular geographic areas) may provide substantial benefits and warrant the use of several different vendors. Since there may be a conflict between the requirements of some special services provided by agents and those of subscription handling, libraries will have to weigh the trade-offs in their own situations.

A final overall consideration is whether it is preferable to have agents interface with libraries' software and hardware or have libraries use the agents' software and hardware. As explained in the discussion of the two different kinds of check-in assistance available, this really depends on the existing automation support available to libraries. Use of an agent's system might actually create work for the automated library, but it could be the most desirable alternative for a small unautomated library with access to relatively inexpensive labor for serials processing.

In approaching the serials services available from subscription agents, librarians need to think positively and creatively. Partial, hybrid, or interim solutions are better than no solutions at all. Even if the precise service package suitable to a specific library's needs is not available today, there is no reason why it could not be available tomorrow. Some existing serial processing services were developed simply because NLM needed them and was willing to spend time and energy persuading agents to attempt them. Convincing some of them was not easy, but, to use an inelegant phrase, subscription agents are on the hook now. They are interested and are developing exciting new services on their own. They are receptive to new ideas, and a library which has one may have a chance to get in on the ground floor and assist in the development of a service ideally suited to its needs.

REFERENCES

1. See description by Martha Fishel and Betsy L. Humphreys in the appendix.

2. Judy Wagner, "Data Base Management System Design for Library Automation," *Journal of Library Automation* 13 (March 1980): 56-60.

3. F. F. Clasquin, "Periodical Prices 1977-79 Update," *Library Journal* 104 (Oct. 15, 1980): 2168-71. This is one recent article.

Available Automated Check-in Systems: A Panel Discussion

Moderator: WILLIAM GRAY POTTER

Mr. Potter: The members of the panel represent organizations that are actively marketing or will soon be marketing a check-in system. I should stress that some of the other exhibitors at this institute are also offering their systems for replication. For example, Northwestern has had its system replicated at the National Library of Venezuela and is also negotiating with the University of Florida. UCLA has seen its system transferred to the University of Alabama Medical Library in Birmingham. These institutions and other nonprofit exhibitors have systems that might be purchased or leased.

Each of the panelists has received a list of six topics which I would like each of them to discuss. After we have gone through these topics, there will be time for questions from the audience.

First, I would like each of the panelists to give us a brief overview of the major features of his system. We will start with Mr. Stephens.

Mr. Stephens: EBSCO is pleased to have the occasion of this meeting of LITA to introduce our online serials control system. This system has been in development by cooperation with a medium-sized health science library for about the last year or so and is based on an earlier version of the UCLA Biomedical Serials

William Gray Potter is Acquisitions Librarian, University of Illinois, Urbana-Champaign; Jim Stephens, president of EBSCO; Jerry Lowell, deputy director of the Research and Development Division of Faxon; Ronald Gardner, instructional coordinator of the User Services Division, OCLC; and Millard F. Johnson, research associate in Machine Methods at Washington University, representing PHILSOM.

Program. This library has used the system for almost five years. The system will be available for formal presentation and demonstration to interested parties by the second quarter of 1981 and available for installation by the third quarter of 1981.

In giving an overview, I would like to mention some of the major characteristics. First, the system is designed for any serially received information, regardless of the medium or regardless of the source. Second, any teletype terminal or any IBM 3278 terminal can be used with the system. Third, the system is available to our subscription customers or noncustomers. Fourth, security for the system is by user number and by terminal number. Fifth, the records are maintained in our computer files. They are accessed online through TYMNET's data communication lines and their software. There is an alternative to TYMNET. The alternative is a dedicated line, used where the volume of usage is enough at a single institution or a group of institutions in geographic proximity and where a dedicated line also results in a lower communication cost than through TYMNET. There are six major functions in the system. These are check-in, bindery, claiming, invoice payment reference, full record display, and a public reference display. There are over fifty information elements that have been identified and assigned within the system, and the system has the flexibility to receive more information elements if there is a demand for them.

Through a set of bibliographic identifiers, the system is programmed to update records or to expose records to review for various functions automatically. The automatic features mainly relate to those tasks dealing with serials that are clerically repetitive. For example, there is a prediction of the next expected issue in the check-in routine. There is an automatic updating of the bindery file when a shipment is returned from the binder which produces a bindery history note and at the same time updates the holdings record. There is an automatic updating of the holdings record at the time of check-in. So there are automatic features built into the system to lessen the amount of clerical effort in the mechanical tasks of doing repetitive functions.

One of the most versatile and helpful features in the system is a very flexible method of accessing or retrieving records. Records can be retrieved by unique identifiers, such as ISSN or our title number. If the library has an identifier assigned to each title, that can be used. The publisher's subscription number, which is typically the string of characters on the top of the mailing lable, can also be used to retrieve. Identifiers which are occasionally common, such as words from a title, can be used to call up the records. Identifiers which are very often common, such as LC class number, Dewey Decimal number, or a subject word, can be used to bring up records. After an identifier is entered, a list appears on the screen. This list may contain one or many records. If it is a unique identifier, you can get one. If it is less unique, you may get several. These are numbered and if you wish to go to the record of one of the titles, you put in the number beside the title and it takes you to that record.

Mr. Lowell: Faxon's automated serials check-in system provides libraries with online access to Faxon's computer facilities where each library's check-in file is stored. The check-in system is designed to handle all of the library's currently received titles, whether they are ordered direct, gifts, exchanges, or vendor placed. The basic record for each title in a library's check-in file consists of two screens.

Screen one contains the current check-in matrix. The matrix consists of columns that in most cases correspond to a year and rows under each column that reflect the number of pieces received during that year. Linked to each row is a system supplied date. The rows of the matrix can either contain volume issue information, reflecting the issue being checked in, or a two-character status code covering nonreceipt occurrences, such as "WL" for want listings, "C1" for first claims, etc.

Screen two includes detailed information on missing issues being claimed, replaced, want listed, etc., and a comments area for local library use. Both screens contain a wide variety of additional data necessary for effective serials processing and management, including call number, shelving location, current issue location, routing and marking instructions, holdings, frequency, issues per year, ISSN, Library of Congress classification, index and abstracting codes, binding instructions, etc. Screens three and following will contain previous years' check-in matrixes.

Access to each library's check-in file will be through the following search capabilities: a title-alpha search on Faxon's title, on an alternate access point selected by the library, or on a cataloged entry input by the library when such entry differs from Faxon's choice; ISSN; the Faxon title number; the library's call number; or a local ID number if used by the check-in library, such as an OCLC, WLN, RLIN, UTLAS, or local system number.

One of the major features of Faxon's serials check-in service is its claim warning system. Faxon will be handling all claims activity for the Faxon-placed titles. Numerous batch reports are generated as part of the check-in service. These reports may be used in public service, collection development, management, or financial capacities. The following batch reports are routinely issued: monthly master lists, which include the majority of data contained on screens one and two sorted by title, available on microfiche or hard copy print-out; bi-weekly Faxon activity reports indicating action that Faxon has taken on each customer's check-in file; and monthly check-in statistics reflecting analysis of the number of titles on the check-in file and the number of issues received, claims entered, and claims outstanding.

Other batch reports are available on request. These include master lists sorted by fields other than title; publication status lists, which could indicate, for example, all temporarily suspended titles; lists based on format, for example, all microform titles; and status code lists, such as titles containing want listed or replacement issue orders.

Another important feature of Faxon's serials check-in system is that other Faxon files will be available to remote access check-in libraries. These include the Faxon Title File containing valuable bibliographic and financial data; the Publisher File; the History File, giving the specific historical/financial data for each library's order for titles placed through Faxon; SCAN, providing a library with the invoice, page, and line number for its Faxon-placed titles; and TWIP, which is the file that lists titles within publisher. Part of the security system for check-in allows each individual library to determine whether it wishes other libraries to have display only access to its check-in records. Libraries will therefore be able to have online access to other libraries' check-in data if these libraries have authorized such display.

Lastly, an electronic mail box system will be available to remote access check-in users that will provide online message switching capabilities between the library and Faxon. This electronic mail box can be used for ordering, claiming, requests for adjustments, or for specific questions.

Mr. Gardner: OCLC services are based on member participation through use of the cataloging subsystem. The cooperative venture of contributing to the online union catalog is the foundation from which other subsystems operate. The serials control subsystem works from this principle. Bibliographic records for serials are selected from the online union catalog. Basic bibliographic information is system supplied and added to a serial control local data record. The user completes a local data record with any local data that is deemed necessary. In setting up serial local data records, certain fields are prepared for the check-in capability. Library personnel receiving serial issues check them against the appropriate serial local data record. With received or missing information, the terminal operator performs several tasks with which the system then will completely update the record.

The union listing capability will provide an additional enhancement to the serials control subsystem. Non-OCLC members may have data input via union list agents, and OCLC members may input their own union listings data or also go through a union list agent. The American National Standard Institute ANSI Z39.42 standard "Serial Holdings Statements at the Summary Level" will be employed. Input of data into the serial local data record is required only once for one or more union list groups, but the display of this information will be system supplied in as many union list groups in which a library participates. Any authorized serials control user may search any of the union list groups. For those without online access to OCLC, there will be offline products.

A most significant feature about the serials control subsystem is the flexibility it provides each library in setting up local serial records and the fact that these records are built upon the CONSER bibliographic records.

Mr. Johnson: PHILSOM is a network; the acronym means Periodical Holdings of Libraries of Schools of Medicine, and by that we mean it is generally intended for medical school libraries. We have fifteen libraries in the network at this time and approximately another fifteen in the previous version of PHILSOM at the Medical Library Center of New York.

PHILSOM accepts libraries either as batch mode libraries or as online libraries. Batch mode libraries participate by pulling receipt cards from a file of expected receipts and by coding forms for data not predictable and new titles. These are sent to PHILSOM headquarters where they are key punched and entered into the system. Online libraries participate either by having a terminal to the PHILSOM headquarters library or by having a minicomputer in their own library or near their own library which they can share with other libraries. This is called a distributed computer system, and the advantages of this distributed system is that there are no telecommunications costs associated with it.

We have two types of data in the PHILSOM system. Basic data, which is generally the data about the journal regardless of which library holds it, is entered at the PHILSOM headquarters using the standard of the Medical Library Center of New York and their union catalog of periodicals. All libraries receiving new titles or spotting title changes send that information with verification to the PHILSOM headquarters where any disagreements between libraries are resolved in favor of our arbitrary standard. Location data is maintained by the local library and is completely the responsibility of the local library. This includes the set or subscription number, holdings, routing, latest issue received, shelving, binding information, subject codes, and any fiscal data.

Mr. Potter: Our next question gets to the heart of the matter and that is: How will libraries pay to use these systems? We are not after specific pricing, but we want to know what the pricing structure will be.

Mr. Lowell: The recurring monthly charge for Faxon's serials check-in system is based on four components. The first is equipment charges, which covers terminals. A library may acquire their own hardware or lease such hardware from Faxon. The second aspect is line charges, which we hope to prorate on a per terminal basis based on geographic location and linked to the first digit of the zip code. Third is the monthly base fee, linked to the number of check-in records on the specific customer's file. The monthly base fee provides for an established number of transactions to cover check-in, claiming activity, and access to the file for collection management and public service purposes. And finally, a transaction fee which will be assessed when the check-in library uses more transactions than allowed as part of the monthly based fee. The equipment and line charges do not contain any Faxon profit, overhead, or development costs. They are simply costs transmitted back to the library. An initial nonrecurring charge is assessed the library to load the check-in file. A Faxon-placed title is less expensive to load than a non-

Faxon-placed title since the Faxon-placed titles can be automatically loaded into the check-in file by using the Faxon invoice information which is stored on Faxon's computer.

Mr. Gardner: The OCLC charges are passed on to regional networks which in turn charge participating libraries. Each network determines the additional charges if any which will be added to the basic OCLC charges for their services. There are charges related to the cataloging system, and each charge is determined again by the network and how it will be passed to participating libraries. The serials control subsystem charges are based on transactions that occur within that subsystem — namely, check-in, union listing, and claiming. At this time check-in charges are minimal, and it is the only charge that is passed on to our users currently. Charges have not been determined for union listing and claiming capability, but the per transaction charge is most likely the type of charge that will be passed on when these enhancements are added to the serials control subsystem.

Mr. Johnson: There are several components of charging for PHILSOM. When a library joins the network, there is an entrance fee, which covers the cost of the network coordinator to come and train the library staff in the usage of the system, and for batch mode libraries it includes all the key punching associated with entering data. For online libraries there is a hardware cost of at least one terminal and one printer. After the library is in the system, the recurring product costs are intended to be based on the amount of the system resources which are used. We charge directly for products. If a library produces a lot of lists on expensive media, they will pay proportionately higher than a library that chooses to use simple computer print-outs or a small number of lists. We also produce output on microfilm, and we will send magnetic tapes to libraries that wish to use their own computer center to print output. Then there is an overhead fee that we divide among the libraries in a network to pay for our personnel costs associated with running the network. This is based on the number of active and inactive sets held by the library. Finally, libraries that are online pay their own telecommunications costs. In the distributed mode, the library with its own minicomputer or which uses one in a consortium effort pays for its use of that minicomputer.

Mr. Stephens: With respect to the cost of the EBSCO system, a couple of general comments. We have no operating experience with this system, that is, we do not have ten libraries now that are online to our computer center and have been operating with it for awhile. So I think that it should be recognized that the pricing situation now with a lack of operating experience is a difficult one. We recognize that it is a difficult one, and I would imagine that most others that will offer systems will agree. In looking at a serials online system, the situation has a certain nature which suggests that economies of scale and volume of activity will enable those who are offering systems to lower their costs if they can get the volume. We have looked and said what if after one year we have three libraries that are on this, in the second year we get three more, and the third year we get three more? What do we lose as we move along as compared with what the situation would be if we had ten the first year and had the revenue from those ten immediately coming in. Offering a serials online system entails a significant upfront investment, and it also entails many fixed costs in that you have to support and support well the system whether you have one customer using it or whether you have twenty customers using it. So given the upfront costs and the fixed costs, volume will play a big factor in what pricing will do in the future.

We have opted for a straightforward and simple pricing system. We will have a cost for the use of the entire system. You can use it to your heart's content. There are a number of printing programs connected with it, and you can do a great variety of things with our system that you will only be able to understand after a full presentation. You can do as much of this as you wish for a fixed fee per year per title checked-in. And there will be a significantly smaller cost per year per title for the record that is not checked in. And this is one of two components. The second component is the communication cost. If TYMNET is used, the cost will vary by location between $5 and $17 per hour. The alternate to TYMNET is to have a dedicated line if the volume usage is there. We estimate that a library using this system will be connected a maximum of thirty-two hours per month to a minimum of fifteen hours per month per 1,000 titles checked in. The cost to the library is a factor of the number of titles and the number of hours it takes to process those titles. On that cost there will be no social security taxes, no group insurance. However, as human beings can get sick or occasionally not come to work, computers sometimes fail and this is known as "down time." If you have down time, it will be most likely to occur when the university president comes by the first time to see the new toy.

Mr. Potter: I would now like each of the panelists to discuss how their system does handle or will handle claims.

Mr. Gardner: Claiming, which is being completed and prepared for installation, is the latest of the serials control enhancements at OCLC. The serials local data record is being modified and expanded to include new requirements for the claiming capability. A definition field currently in use is to be expanded to allow users a great deal of control over predicted issues and their receipt. A user will be able to receive and/or claim every issue if the title is at all regular. Both the claiming and check-in features will be able to use and benefit from this change. The addition of a purchase field will allow the user to enter data about purchasing and invoicing, such as purchase order number, invoice number, and related dates. These elements are used to supply information that will be printed on the offline claim notice. A claims field will allow the user to identify a claim mode of automatic, semi-automatic, or manual. The number of claim cycles is user selected, and other features are user input. The OCLC name address directory will be used to find appropriate control numbers which in turn will be combined with the claims field to direct where the claim forms are sent and where replies are also to be sent. Several management files will be added to the online files for each institution. Both check-in and claiming will benefit from a user defined periodical frequency capability. Most important is the fact that an automated monitoring system will be in place so that a library may have improved inventory control of its entire serial collection.

Mr. Johnson: We have two types of claims in PHILSOM. The first type asks for any issue that has been skipped in check-in. The second type of claim is what we call a late issue warning, and it is for any title that has not come in after a specified amount of time. In the batch mode system, claims are produced once each month as a part of the batch update. The late issue warnings are produced on the basis of a generalized algorithm which takes into account the frequency of a journal and when it was last received. We also note the date the publisher expects to publish any individual issue, so if a publisher publishes an annual in January, a claim would be generated in February. In the online system, you are notified of a claim immediately if an issue is skipped, and it goes into the print queue to be printed later. The library sets a number of days that are allowed to elapse after the last receipt of a journal before a warning is produced. These claims and warnings are produced as a separate function which prints out a list in order of vendor and alphabetically within vendor as a part of the claim and warning function. We found it would be irresponsible to mail out claims without some manual intervention and checking into the accuracy of claims.

Mr. Stephens: Claiming starts in the EBSCO system with check-in. If the check-in clerk is sitting at the terminal and has in hand the *Journal of East European History,* the first job is to bring up the check-in screen. And if I were the check-in clerk, I would do it by keying in two words, East and History. The file will be searched to identify all titles that contain those words, and if there is more than one title, they would be displayed in list form. Let's say that three were displayed that had the two words East and History in their title. If the one you were looking for was number two, you would then key two, and it would bring up the check-in screen for that title which would have the record elements that are pertinent to the check-in process. One of the top lines on the screen would have a line where the next issue that should be received has been predicted. Not every issue can be predicted. Somebody said yesterday that maybe 70 percent of the titles in one file could be predicted. The prediction will indicate the year, the volume number, the issue number, and the issue date. If this is the item in hand, then the check-in clerk will key "yes" and the title will be checked in. If the issue in hand is not the one that the system has predicted, then you key in the issue that you have in hand and at that point you have two options. You can go to a claim format and generate a claim. We print and mail claims to publishers two times per week. If you do not wish to generate a claim immediately, you have the choice of letting the existence of that gap go into a claim file. It will go into the claim file and be there for you to review.

At this point, I would like to mention irregulars, one of the most challenging problems in claims. All irregulars are identified as such in the record. For every title that is in your file, you can indicate a number of months allowance over which nonreceipt is acceptable. For irregulars, if you do not indicate a particular number of months, the system allows six months. What this says is, if there is no receipt of that title within six months, then a record will automatically go into the claim file so you can look at it and decide whether to claim.

The contents of the claim file are all outstanding claims. It will indicate whether a title has been claimed two or three times or what the status is. The claim file is a review file. When you want to work it, you work it. You sit down and go through it. There will be a number of options for what you page through to review and work. If you choose to sit down with the claim file and look only at irregulars, then you can page through the irregulars which have been put into the files since you last worked the files. If you wish to sit down and bring up for review only those items which have already been claimed two times, to decide whether to send a third claim, then you can select those items and look at those. There are two records connected with claims that are important and are displayed on most screens you look at. One is claim notes in which you can put any miscellaneous comments. Another one is a claim history note, which has a record of everything that is an outstanding claim.

In summary, the two most important features are first, the automatic identification of a gap or of a title which simply ceases to come, and second, that the system is built on a claim file which is available for you to review. If you choose not to review and want to claim immediately, you can do this at the point of check-in. A manual claim can be made at any time.

Mr. Lowell: Faxon's claims warning system is designed to routinely scan a check-in customer's file to select and print out those title records which possibly need claiming action because of lapses, gaps, or delinquent first, second, or third claims.

The gaps portion of the claims warning system covers gaps when the subscription is still arriving but specific issues were not received. The selection of the title appearing on this list is triggered by a CG or claim a gap status code input into the check-in matrix when a check-in operator discovers a gap because of a missing issue.

The lapses portion of the claims warning system covers subscriptions that totally stop coming or have never started arriving. Selection of titles for the lapses report is based on an arrival number factor, one of the fields contained on the check-in screen. This arrival number is the number of days that the system will allow to lapse between check-in activity from line to line within the check-in matrix. An important feature of the Faxon check-in system is that this arrival number is linked to each specific customer's check-in record for a specific title and can be changed by the check-in library to reflect its receipt patterns for this title.

The delinquent first, second, and third claims portion of the claims warning system contains titles whose first, second, or third claims are older than fifty-six days. Claims warning system print-outs are issued in duplicate. Faxon's remote access check-in department will keep one copy and handle all claims work required for all titles placed through Faxon, with the exception of the delinquent third claims since these titles will no longer automatically be monitored by the system.

Faxon claims activity on behalf of the client will be immediately reflected on the customer's check-in file. The check-in library will receive the other copy of the claims print-out and will process claims as required, updating the check-in files as appropriate for those titles not placed through Faxon. The gaps report will be issued weekly; the lapses and delinquent first, second, and third claims reports will be issued biweekly. In addition an "irregulars to be reviewed" report will appear every six months containing titles with irregular frequencies that have not had any check-in activity during the previous six months. This report will be mailed directly to the check-in library, which will be responsible for processing all claims for irregular titles regardless of the source.

Mr. Potter: Each of these check-in systems is a part of a larger serial control system. The next question that I would like each of the panelists to address is how does the serial check-in system fit into his overall system for serials management?

Mr. Johnson: Check-in is central to the PHILSOM system. In batch mode libraries, we mail out a set of prepunched receipt cards representing items that are expected to be received in the following month. We have been doing this a long time, and we probably have reliability of better than 80 percent, probably up to 90 percent, but nobody can stop a publisher from changing his title. For those titles for which there is no prepunched card, the serials librarian fills out one line on a form and then mails the form to PHILSOM headquarters for updating.

Now, we have designed the online system primarily from the point of view of check-in, and the first activity is to find the title. The librarian can find the title to be checked in by keying in either the title number that has been assigned by PHILSOM, the ISSN from the journal, or a search key that is the first two characters of the first four words in the title, significant or nonsignificant. Response time is very fast, a matter of seconds, and the display will be the full title of the journal, the routing code, the action code, and the entire holdings of the library complete to each individual issue. The computer then will tell the librarian what issue is expected next. If the librarian has that issue she types "Y" and return. If she has the same volume, but a different issue, she types in only the issue number, and the holding string is updated and displayed. If she has a different volume and a different issue, she types in the volume number, a slash, and then the issue number.

Mr. Stephens: The check-in system is, of course, the heart of the online serials control activity. The question was asked yesterday, is it faster to check in online than it is to check in manually? I think it is a little bit faster. It is a faster mechanical process than what I understand goes on with a manual check-in system. In the EBSCO system, you can bring up a check-in screen as I described earlier by keyword input. The system has predicted the issue which should arrive if it is predictable, and there is a simple command to check in if that issue has arrived, which will happen in most cases.

The check-in system interfaces with claiming to identify a gap. Also, it interfaces with claiming by reading the date last received plus the number of months that you have put in as an allowance for nonreceipt, to put into the claim file for review any title in the system you need to claim it because it simply stopped coming. This is an easier production of a claim mechanically, in my opinion, than probably what is done in most libraries now, whether you are handwriting a postcard and dropping it in the mail or sitting down at the typewriter and typing a claim form or whatever. The system identifies a title that is ready to be bound and automatically puts this into a bindery file which you then review and can instruct to proceed to produce bindery slips and go through the bindery process. And I think that this is probably a faster routine than what takes place now. Check-in is the heart and if it interfaces with these other activities, it is a neater, cleaner operation than what exists with a manual system.

Mr. Lowell: As Faxon's serials check-in system has been designed and implemented, the needs of overall serials control and management have been continuously considered. Many of the fields that are contained on the check-in system were initially included because they are needed for proper and effective serials management. The batch reports that are produced as part of the check-in service can be extremely helpful in the areas of fiscal control and collection development. Monthly statistical reports can be helpful in assessing labor requirements for serial units. Other reports can be useful in public service capacities. Effective claims processing as a result of the claims warning system generates a higher level of receipt of issues ordered without the added monetary cost associated with purchasing replacement copies when claims were not processed on time. In addition, and more importantly, perhaps, the availability of the other Faxon files containing bibliographic and financial data enhances the actual serials check-in system since such online access is most important for serials management.

Faxon has several planned enhancements for serials check-in which directly relate to the total serials management picture. These include an automated routing subsystem, a binding module, and a financial acquisition subsystem to more completely monitor serials purchasing and fund encumbering.

Mr. Gardner: Total serials management has become more important in all libraries. With the serials budget climbing faster and consuming more of the total library budget in many institutions, better serials management is required. The OCLC serials control subsystem provides the capability for online inventory control of all serials. Bibliographic control through the online union catalog provides access to over 300,000 serial records of which over 250,000 are CONSER records. The check-in capability already exists and is being successfully used in more than seventy-five libraries. The serials local data record provides many variable fields for the user. The user sets up the check-in fields by defining the various parts of the serial and by predicting the next expected issue. When this is done, the terminal operator again receives or misses an issue by simply typing appropriate commands for the issues that are received. Any serials with regular issues can be effectively handled in this manner. With the claiming capability enhancements forthcoming, a better way of handling more serials on an automatic basis will be present for OCLC participants. A means for the user to establish when an issue is expected will be provided. Both check-in and claiming will benefit. The union listing capability is scheduled for installation this fall and will fit into total serials control. Data for union listing is input into the same serial local data record and is maintained by each OCLC library or by an agent for the nonparticipating OCLC library. A library may belong to as many union list groups as deemed necessary. A display for each group is provided to the serials control subsystem subscribers. Union listing provides the means for better interlibrary ventures, including cooperative acquisitions and interlibrary loan. Acquisitions is to be linked to the serials control subsystem in the future. At present, serials may be ordered but no linkage exists between the two subsystems. So with all the various parts available to a library, serials management may include a wide management spectrum from acquisitions, to check-in, claiming, and union listing.

Mr. Potter: I would now like the panelists to discuss how the application of his system might vary as to size of library.

Mr. Stephens: Basically, it does not vary with the size of the library. I think it is as applicable for a smaller library as it is for a very large library. I would like to comment that if there is a library that would like to have the EBSCO system on the university computer, we are prepared and happy to talk with you and the university computer center to make the system available. Also, we are investigating the development of a system which could be put on a minicomputer which could be in the library that we would market as a piece of software. We have not been able to make a decision as to whether we want to go forward and put the investment in it, but we are investigating.

Mr. Lowell: The application of Faxon's check-in system does not vary as to size of library. All libraries, regardless of library size, use the same core check-in system. Each library may tailor use of fields within the system to its unique environment, but this flexibility of use by each library is not necessarily a function of size. For example, if the library does not classify its journals, the call number field on Faxon's check-in system can be used to contain other data, a powerful flexibility in that the call number field is searchable on line. Some aspects of the system may tend to limit usage depending on the size of the library. For example, the current system is designed for dedicated line usage only with remote terminals linked to the computer in Westwood, Massachusetts. The resulting equipment and line charges may be prohibitive for smaller sized libraries.

Mr. Gardner: The size of a library or its serial collection has very little to do in determining a library's application of the OCLC's serials control subsystem. The serial local data record has been designed to allow each user the greatest amount of flexibility possible. So each library in the end determines what is required for an online file of serials control records. A major consideration for each library is the time, staff, and cost required to convert from any manual file to an online file. There have been a range of libraries that have made the transition, some with serial collections of approximately 600 titles to major libraries with over 60,000 serial titles. The majority have between 1,000 and 5,000 titles.

A recent development removes one process which has slowed conversion. Two transactions have been required to establish a serial local data record, first in the cataloging subsystem and then in the serials control subsystem. The user now has an option of going directly into the serials control subsystem and selecting bibliographic records to create serial local data records and to attach a holding symbol to the appropriate bibliographic record. This will be advantageous to those libraries who do not "catalog" the serial in their collection. Existing and newly implemented features are designed for all sizes of institutions, and it is hoped that serials control is provided to all sizes of libraries through the present system design and that future enhancements will improve the management of serials.

Mr. Johnson: The libraries in our network do not vary greatly in size, from about 1,500 titles to 6,000 at the most. We don't respond to differences in size, but we do respond drastically to differences in demands and demands can be stated as resources. In other words, we give rich libraries a lot more than we give the poor libraries. To go first class in PHILSOM, you would be online using long line telecommunications and would get your batch mode outputs on our most expensive medium, which is a nicely printed page. You might have more work copies spread around your library. We would program special modules for your library to produce exactly what you want. Our program is very modular, and we do this on a regular basis even for the poorer libraries. They would probably be in a batch mode, which is a less costly method of networking, and they would normally get their output on magnetic tape and load it on their own computer and print it out on computer paper with fewer copies. So we range not so much in the size of the library but in the resources a library can expend on serials control.

Mr. Potter: Finally, I would like each of the panelists to discuss the potential of his system for interfacing with other systems, for example, locally developed systems, bibliographic utilities, etc.

Mr. Lowell: One of the fields on Faxon's check-in system is called

ID number. The ID number field is designed to contain a unique title identifier number used by a local in-house system or a title or identifier number used by one of the major networks. Through the use of this number it is possible to develop, at the local level, programs that would combine check-in data from the Faxon check-in system with data contained in bibliographic systems at this local level. Check-in data could also be used in circulation systems through the use of this ID number field. We would ideally like to see the bulk of check-in processing activity occurring at the local site rather than on our mainframe in Westwood. Under this ideal environment, a distributed network would reduce workload on the mainframe and would still provide contact with the host computer facility for other files and data not available at the local site. However, our experience has thus far been with mainframe processing, and we therefore have started with a central network.

Faxon is also pursuing the potential of linkage with the major bibliographic utilities or the regional affiliated networks to enable these systems to access the Faxon check-in service and our related automated files. The development status of such linkage varies between the bibliographic utilities. Faxon would like to be able to use existing networks and hardware already available within the library rather than instituting yet another network and another set of terminal requirements at the local library. On the other hand, Faxon is pursuing this linkage potential with caution. There are legal and tax implications that exist with for-profit institutions working with not-for-profit institutions. Faxon also does not want to restrict future development by locking itself in with one or more of the existing networks and tying its future to the future of the network.

Mr. Gardner: Interfacing of computer systems has been and will be of interest to librarians. On the outside, many similarities exist between systems, and questions arise from librarians asking can this be done or can that be done? Almost every response is "Yes, technically, such and such can be done, but . . ." That inevitable conjunction pops up. Most automated library systems are still fairly young. If you will, they are just reaching adolescence. Each company or library still must confront the daily requirements of their own computer services, and the maintenance and development required result in inordinate amounts of time and money.

Of course, some interfacing already exists between OCLC and

the Library of Congress, the National Library of Medicine, and the National Library of Canada. However, most of these processes are batch. Two other cooperative adventures of interest include the Government Printing Office, which utilizes OCLC to create the monthly catalog, and a recent grant awarded to OCLC and the Research Libraries Group for a study of the approaches, problems, and the priorities involved in developing online patron access to bibliographic databases. One specific project which points the way toward an interactive and dynamic system is the CONSER project. This cooperative effort to build a machine-readable database of serials encompasses many types of libraries.

OCLC has begun a project to test a remote communications processor. This type of computer interfacing may prove to be a step forward in the evolution of library-related automation and may have an impact on all sizes and types of libraries. The need to allow the computer of one system to communicate with another system's computer becomes a key element in any cooperative venture. As the costs of serials and maintenance of these serials continue to rise sharply, interfacing of computers will become a necessity and ultimately will provide another means of keeping library expenses down. Locally, libraries have the option to acquire a machine-readable tape of their cataloging activities to interface with their own system's needs. Union lists will also provide a tape product for local use.

OCLC is continuing the exploration and experimental stages of interfacing with local, regional, national, and international library and information related computer services to provide better ways of handling the data that libraries need from day to day. Cooperative ventures have been a part of OCLC's past and present and will continue in the future.

Mr. Johnson: We feel that our future is in the medical library community, which has a long history of detailed networking. We would definitely like to get our authoritative bibliographic data from a national medical periodicals database when one is established and maintained, probably by the National Library of Medicine. At the lower end, we would like to interface PHILSOM with minicomputer integrated library systems, such as that being developed by the Lister Hill Center of the National Library of Medicine. We would like to see PHILSOM become one of the sources which can act in distributing the product of a national medical periodicals database and, ultimately, a national periodicals database. I think that is the way we would like to see networking go. In conjunction with networking, I really feel that the greatest contribution which PHILSOM can make to the whole library community is to be a prototype for distributed networks of the future. In that context, I have in the past contacted every organization on this podium and some of the commercial firms that offer distributed circulation systems. I am hoping something will come of that in the future.

Mr. Stephens: In the EBSCO system, there are plenty of identifiers that exist whereby two records could be tied together. We have assigned a very low priority to considerations of interfacing because our little network has no members now, and we think it will be a little while before we have very many. We recognize the ultimate aim of being able to interface and we intend over time to be in a position to respond to that.

Mr. Potter: At this time, I would like to open this session for questions from the floor.

Joe Chervenak, Solar Energy Research Institute: I have a general question for all the panelists. Typically, in most libraries, there are a number of processing steps that take place after check-in. What I am thinking of are mailing labels, routing slips, cataloging decision slips, call number labels, and so forth. To what extent do your systems plan to deal with these tasks which seem to be very open to be automated.

Mr. Gardner: OCLC has defined some of these same needs which you have pointed out. Some people have made use of the existing serials control subsystems for routing information by using one of our remarks fields. In terms of providing this on an automated basis, future enhancements being discussed and talked about will include more of these kind of things for label production, routing slip production, and so forth.

Mr. Johnson: PHILSOM has an interface with the circulation system in development now whereupon we put a bar-code on the item at check-in time, but we really don't do very much for what you are talking about.

Mr. Stephens: The EBSCO system contains a routing code and a location code, and these can be used to handle the issue. I think there is a lot of variability as to what people do. What we would plan to do is to talk with a customer and find out what they want. The printer, which we definitely think should be right there with the system, could be used to produce print-outs or labels.

95

Mr. Lowell: As the Faxon system is currently designed and operational, the majority of work which you describe would still be manual. The fields are there to contain the data, but there is no mechanism for an offline printer to produce a label containing the data on that field. The only one that probably will be changing very shortly would be a routing slip. We have done that because we feel, especially in the corporate library environment, that automated routing slip production is a very high priority item.

Mr. Chervenak: I have a second question. Do the systems described allow for a centralized check-in facility which many libraries do utilize? If you are checking in twenty copies for a main branch and several copies for other branches, it significantly increases the size of the record.

Mr. Johnson: No, we don't do that at PHILSOM.

Mr. Stephens: I think that, as I understand the question, you would have different location codes and possibly you would have each record in the file, and you could check in each one on the EBSCO system.

Mr. Lowell: There is nothing to stop you from having decentralized check-in with the Faxon system. You would have to pay for a terminal at each site doing decentralized check-in. The security system could then allow only your set of libraries to look at each other's records. As regards your example of the twenty copies, you can elect if you wish to check in all twenty copies on one master screen or have twenty different records for checking in those twenty copies. If you lump everything together on one screen, however, you have lost all the copy specific control within the other fields on the check-in record.

Mr. Gardner: The OCLC system also provides for lumping together all copies and, as Mr. Lowell said, you lose that specificity in controlling each copy. You may centrally receive all issues and then disperse them or, if you want, you may have remote check-in capabilities at any branch library, either through a direct access through your dedicated line or by dial access.

Richard Meyer, Clemson University: I have sort of a three-part question for Jim Stephens, but Mr. Lowell, if you can shed some light on this, please do. As I understood you, you said that EBSCO estimated that it would take fifteen to thirty-two hours per month per 1,000 titles to utilize the system per terminal. Can you tell us how you arrived at that estimate?

Mr. Stephens: We arrived at the estimate by the actual usage of the system by the library that we have been working with plus some observations by ourselves on how they did it. We think they can do certain things faster than they do.

Mr. Meyer: There are about 170 hours available in the month. Somewhere around 5,000 titles, then, might require more than one terminal. How does someone go about predicting how many terminals they are going to need?

Mr. Stephens: My answer to that is that you do it, and as soon as you see that you need a second terminal, you hook a second terminal up. That is a possible answer to the previous question. If you are checking in at one location for several locations, then the answer I made applies. If you check in at three locations on your campus, you need three terminals. And more terminals can be added easily.

Mr. Lowell: Given the difference of the configuration of the network, Faxon is not basing hardware requirements on hours. Our statistical work and our equipment predictions are based on 4,000 titles per terminal per person and that is based on the average of ten issues per year per title. If your collection consists of many monographic series and irregulars which would reduce that ten pieces a year average, then likewise your 4,000 titles per terminal per person can go up to 6,000 titles per terminal per person. That is the range that we are using, 4,000 to 6,000 titles for a terminal for one person.

Elizabeth Kelley, Southern Illinois University Law School: I would like to hear any of your panelists comment on the adaptability of their systems to check-in and claim government issued serials received through a depository program.

Mr. Gardner: You receive your items and check them in one by one. However, it has been something OCLC has looked into. I don't know where we are going with it, but we are trying to work with depository libraries in setting up some capability so that we can identify pieces coming on a regular basis so that they could all be received in a bundle, if you will. But right now, you receive the bundle, you break it apart, and check them in one by one.

Barbara Moore, University of Wisconsin, Whitewater: From listening to other presentations, it seems to me there are few libraries in the country that do have fully automated serial check-in systems. Some are in the process of being developed and some are not complete. My question to you is, what is a good estimate for when we can expect full serial automated check-in systems to come of age?

Mr. Lowell: There might be some ambiguity in determining what is a fully automated serial check-in system. You might disagree, but I think what we are describing comes close. If you mean the latest in issue prediction, the latest in claims immediately going to the publisher with the least amount of human interface, then that is another story. The Faxon system right now is in a test phase from January through May of 1981 and will then be available after that. Test libraries will be using it in January, and our current phase one check-in libraries will be transferred to phase two, which I have been talking about, in November of this year.

Mr. Stephens: I would like to second some thoughts expressed yesterday that there are no technical obstacles, but the obstacles are financial and political, and they contain so many uncertainties that I think it is a very difficult question to answer.

Mr. Gardner: I would agree that it is very difficult to answer. OCLC is looking at an integrated system whereby beginning with the acquisition process through checking in, receiving, union listing, sharing your holdings data, and interlibrary loan, we would like to achieve that kind of integrated serials control. We are moving in that direction. But in terms of a time frame, I really don't know. I think, as pointed out yesterday, many of the problems have been that serials are often pushed to the bottom of the priorities and as libraries have had to fight for the money and the time to handle serials, OCLC has also had some of those problems. We have placed new emphasis on serials control, and we are moving ahead as quickly as we can, so I would hope that over the next few months you will see some dramatic improvement to our subsystem and continue to see enhancements and improvements to serials control.

Mr. Johnson: I would like my colleague Linda Roberts to answer that question.

Ms. Roberts, PHILSOM: I would say that once we begin to use the acquisitions sections, we will have it, or very near to it. It is the last step that we need to get everything we do for serials control in the same system.

Rebecca Lenzini, University of Illinois: As a direct follow-up to that last question, since PHILSOM is a tried and true product which has been around for about seventeen years in its various stages, I wonder if you don't think about expanding it to cover and serve more than just medical libraries? What are some of the difficulties or possibilities there?

Mr. Johnson: We, of course, have thought about it. University libraries, from time to time, have asked to be in PHILSOM, but our position is that that really is not the business we are in. We would be happy to give some consultation, help, or whatever we can give to somebody who would like to expand it. On a further basis, I tried to make the point yesterday that we are not at the end of the technological development. I do not want to be the person to work on PHILSOM IV, but we must certainly realize that the time for the next generation of computer-based systems is here. And the technology is happening incredibly fast.

Mr. Potter: I would like to thank the panelists.

Serials and the Online Catalog

VELMA VENEZIANO

It is axiomatic that automating any aspect of library operations can be justified only if it improves service to the end-user, the library patron. If one ranks various forms of library materials on an ascending scale, starting with those which are most in need of improved access and progressing to those for which access is best, serials stand at the bottom end of the scale and, consequently, the user stands to gain the most if access to them can be improved. But it is not enough just to provide improved access to serials, but better access to all forms of materials. Optimum access is online access, more specifically, access which is a replacement for, not just a supplement to, the card catalog.

Before you can have online patron access, you have to have a database and you have to have a system which operates on that database. How do you get the database and what type of system is necessary in order to provide access to it?

Northwestern has such a database and a system for accessing it. It is hoped that other libraries can benefit from our experience.

THE TOTAL SYSTEMS APPROACH

Northwestern University Library over the last thirteen years has been developing and operating an "online integrated library materials control system." This system is known as NOTIS, short for

Velma Veneziano is library systems analyst at the Northwestern University Library.

Northwestern Online Total Integrated System. We are now in version 3.1 of NOTIS, about to go to version 3.2. NOTIS was developed modularly, starting with circulation, then progressing to cataloging and acquisitions, and, finally, to patron access. Unlike many systems which gave serials short shrift in their initial implementations, serials control (ordering, check-in, claiming, payment posting, cataloging, inventory management, and circulation) was an integral part of our design strategy from the very start. In retrospect, this was a fortunate decision. What we learned is that a system designed to cope with the intricacies of serials can handle monographs with no trouble. It doesn't work the other way around.

The most recent of the NOTIS modules is a patron inquiry capability, which enables patrons to search and display records online. This interface is known as LUIS (short for Library User Information Service). We anticipate that LUIS will enable us to close our card catalog in January 1981.

THE DATABASE

The NOTIS database presently includes all monographs acquired by NUL since 1970, plus our complete serial collection, retrospective as well as current. In 1970, using our shelflist, we mounted a project to convert bibliographic and detailed holdings data for all serials in the library, including monographic series and continuations of monographic sets. Our online bibliographic file consists of about 425,000 records, of which approximately 50,000 are for serials.

To the patron, the system appears to be a "union" file, reflecting not just the Evanston Campus main and branch library materials, but also materials of four other libraries. Each of the participating libraries has its own "file" and does its own ordering and cataloging, creating and modifying its records as necessary. A library wanting to use the cataloging of another library "copies" the record from the source file into its own file where it can be modified or used as is. If a record is modified, both versions of the record are retained in the database. In order to participate in the union file, a library must agree to follow LC, both in forms of names and cataloging rules. Although full level cataloging is encouraged, minimal level cataloging can be accommodated, provided it is properly labeled. Each library has a choice as to type of subject headings used.

FILE AND RECORD STRUCTURE AND CONTENT

Although the internal structure of the online records differs slightly from the structure of the MARC communications format, the system supports all the MARC data elements. Although records may be created and updated online in real time, they can also be created by transferring them in from any tape in MARC communications format. The system, in addition to accepting records in MARC communications format, can produce a "pure" LC/MARC record as output.

All the MARC bibliographic formats (books, serials, music, maps, films, manuscripts) are supported. Very importantly, the MARC authorities format for names and subjects is supported. We also are using a special format based on the draft analytics format which enables indexing and abstracting data for journal literature to be accommodated.

Acquisitions is fully integrated with cataloging. The bibliographic record is created at the point of a decision to acquire a title either by direct keying (using either full or provisional data) or by transfer from the LC/MARC file which we maintain offline. This same bibliographic record eventually becomes the catalog record, updated if necessary by the cataloger. Each bibliographic record is linked to a holdings record, which contains, in addition to certain local title level data, one subrecord (termed a copy statement) for each copy of the title. This copy statement contains copy level status data, (held/not held, single volume/multi-volume, etc.) plus the level and type of cataloging or classification (Dewey/LC, on-order/in-process/cataloged, etc.), plus the location and call number. If "multi-volume" (i.e., a serial or set), each copy statement is linked automatically to a separate "volume holdings" record in which the detailed volume holdings are recorded.

Each copy statement is similarly linked, under machine control, to one or more acquisitions records in which are recorded ordering, receiving, claiming, payment and processing data. Output from the acquisitions module takes a variety of forms. Purchase orders are automatically printed. A flexible claiming capability is provided, for books as well as current issues of serials, triggered by a daily list of records which contain expired action dates. If the listed record is in need of claiming or some other type of follow-up (cancellation, for example), the system has a "customized correspondence generator" which enables a wide variety of letters to vendors to be produced. These letters are all automatically printed, complete with bibliographic and order information, pre-addressed, ready for insertion in window envelopes. Reports of commitments and expenditures, by fund, are produced on a scheduled basis. Each item received by the library, regardless of whether it is a single issue of a periodical or a multi-volume set, is checked in online, providing a completely up-to-the-minute record of all materials received.

As an item received on a standing order basis is checked in, the system automatically assigns a new "action date." If another issue is not received by that date, the record number is listed out on the daily list of expired action dates, and the follow-up routine described above is performed.

Material control does not stop with completion of the acquisitions and cataloging operations. Since the file of bibliographic, holdings, and order records is co-resident with the circulation file, there is continuous control, at the piece level, over almost every item in the collection, even after it leaves the Technical Services Division.

PATRON ACCESS AS AN OUTGROWTH OF MATERIALS MANAGEMENT

For several years after the circulation and technical services systems were installed, there were only terminals in those areas. Gradually, more and more public service terminals were installed. The simplicity and convenience of use led, quite naturally, to the idea that the system, with minimal modification, could be used by the public. When it became apparent that *AACR2* was going to increase the cost of maintaining the card catalog, there developed a sort of grass roots consensus that the natural successor to the card catalog was the online system.

For serials, we were in an excellent position to go this route since almost all titles were already in the database, complete with detailed holdings. The prospect was less encouraging for monographs, with nearly a million unconverted pre-1970 titles. However, to make a long story short, we decided to take the big step and go directly to an online catalog, bypassing COM. A committee was appointed to plan for the changeover, and Kenton Andersen, the library programmer, began the task of designing and programming a user interface which would be a little more "user friendly" than the staff interface and which would consolidate the data displays and put them in a format more intelligible and familiar to users than that used by library staff.

We were also fortunate from a hardware standpoint. In November 1979 we had installed in the library a dedicated IBM 4331 computer to take the place of the IBM 370/138 which we had previously shared with the University Administrative Data Processing Department. The 4331 is a small general purposes computer, which compares very favorably in price with many larger minicomputers. It utilizes the most advanced technology and uses very low-cost, high-density disks. It is extremely reliable. So far we have had an average of only a fraction of a percent of downtime. It enabled us to essentially quadruple our processing power and our storage capacity for about what it previously cost us to buy services on the 370/138.

TESTING THE ONLINE CATALOG

In order to make the changeover as risk-free as possible, our strategy was to operate the online system in parallel with the card catalog until we were sure the system was acceptable to our patrons. We were especially concerned about satisfying the faculty. We planned to use the experimental phase to collect comments from faculty and students so that any flaws could be identified and corrected before closing the catalog. On May 5, 1980, we installed six "patron access" terminals in the card catalog area of the main catalog plus two others in the Science-Engineering and Transportation Libraries. Initially, access was limited to author and title. The test got underway quite smoothly; we mounted a special project with volunteers from the staff working in shifts to assist users and to identify and document problems.

So far, if "use" is any indication, the system is a success. Students walk up to the terminals, read the instructional screen, and proceed to use it with little or no trouble. Their attitude is almost matter-of-fact. This partially may be accounted for by the fact that they had become accustomed to being able to inquire into circulation files and regarded the new system as simply an extension of circulation inquiry. Comments have mostly been enthusiastic. The most common criticism relates to the lack of subject access and the fact that, for books, the database is not inclusive.

Access to serials, for which a subject approach is not as essential, is an unqualified success. A user now knows before going to the stacks or the periodical room not only whether the library has a volume or an issue, but where it is and if it is available. This saves a great deal of time and frustration.

We realize that so far patrons who use the system are self-selected. Confirmed anti-technologists obviously will continue to use the card catalog as long as it is there. But most staff members are confident that, when the planned refinements are implemented, users will be won over by its speed and convenience. We are particularly anxious to get dial-up access installed so faculty can have access from their departmental offices. Although there are inevitable slippages in schedules, we are still optimistic that we can close the card catalog in January 1981, although we will probably maintain a temporary add-on catalog just in case we run into any unanticipated problems.

In the meantime we are developing some additional refinements. The user interface is being made "smarter" and more "user friendly." Our indexes are being improved to permit them to be used for authority control and to supply cross references. We are also developing a two-tiered index structure which will provide subject access without an undue processing load.

COST JUSTIFICATION

A patron access system must have three basic attributes: efficiency (from a machine standpoint); effectiveness (from the patron standpoint); and affordability. Actually, unless a system is efficient and effective, it will not be affordable. In our experience, an efficient, effective, affordable system for patron access requires that bibliographic data be integrated with acquisitions, cataloging, and circulation — in other words it must be part of an overall materials control system. Such a system allows the library to take advantage of the joint principles of "economy of scope" and "economy of scale." A single central processor, using a single set of minimally redundant data records, performing all the basic behind-the-scenes library functions (ordering, check-in, claiming, fund control, cataloging, and circulation, etc.), and which encompasses serials as well as books, can provide direct access for the patron at a fraction of the cost of a dedicated patron access system. In an integrated system, patron access becomes just another view of the database. The transaction load on the system increases, but, since the user and the staff share the same database, there is no additional cost for storage.

Fortunately, the cost of hardware has declined drastically in the last few years. Most medium- to large-size libraries can now easily cost justify a multi-function system, even a library-dedicated one

105

as at NUL. However, a computer in the library is not essential. Libraries can, and in many cases should, consider sharing a computer, either cooperatively with other libraries or with a parent institution. The advantage in sharing is not so much savings in hardware costs as in sharing the costs of software development and maintenance.

Why do I stress the cost of development? In my view there exists no "perfect" library system anywhere at any cost. At this point, libraries wanting online catalogs have two choices: they can acquire a turnkey circulation system which has been beefed up to include bibliographic access or they can look around for a good basic bibliographic system which has the potential for development. Unfortunately, development of any kind, including modification of an existing system, takes time and money and also expertise. This is where the utilities could be doing more than they are. They could be developing software which could be transferred to local computers. What they should not be doing, however, is encouraging libraries to believe that the utility database and system can be used directly as an online catalog.

We are now at the stage where distributed processing is becoming more and more feasible, and this opens up the way for a single large-scale computer (such as that located at a bibliographic utility) to feed bibliographic data to a local computer, not through a black box connected to a terminal screen, but directly computer-to-computer in real time. At Northwestern, we are hoping to work with the Research Libraries Group to develop a means for data to be transmitted directly from the RLIN database into the NOTIS database and conversely.

The reason for reliance on a local system for patron access to catalog data rather than on a bibliographic utility is simple. Patron access requires that a great deal of data be accessed and displayed. If this data has to be transmitted a long distance over communications lines, the telecommunications costs would be substantial and in most cases would outweigh any savings derived from using a central shared facility. Because of the transaction loads involved, I question the feasibility not only of using a remote centralized utility database for catalog access, but also for centralized acquisitions, serials check-in, and circulation. In my opinion, the utilities should stick to what they do best, namely permitting libraries to share cataloging data and the resources represented by that data. Possibly some of the regional networks are logical sites for such services, including patron access, but even here the total number of transactions and the distance from the central computer have to be very carefully studied before a decision can be made. But regardless of where the processing is accomplished — locally, centrally, or distributed between a central and a local site — an integrated, comprehensive materials management system, capable of handling both books and serials, is essential to providing adequate and effective patron access.

Other factors affecting cost and efficiency are the structure of the database, the techniques by which those structures are processed, and the size of the computer on which the processing is performed. I have the strong impression that many libraries have not really thought much about this. They may be very unpleasantly surprised at response time when they begin to use small minicomputers in conjunction with generalized data management systems and inverted file structures under high use conditions.

Most catalogs in large research libraries are heavily used, and there is every indication that online catalogs will be even more heavily used. It is essential that the online catalog be designed to keep performance high by minimizing the number of file accesses. Systems designers, anxious to get something up fast, ignore this principle at their peril. Particularly susceptible to the problem of overload are circulation systems which try to become online catalogs. Many of these systems were built to operate on short records with few access points under relatively small transaction loads. They run into trouble when they start being used as online catalogs, with large numbers of large records with a large number of access points and a large number of simultaneous users.

Before choosing such a system, librarians should make every effort to assure themselves that it will perform under such conditions without response degradation, not just on today's database with today's usage levels, but at the level needed three or four years hence. Any estimates of future use should also take into consideration the increased popularity which will result when the catalog is "distributed" — made available from terminals in remote locations. Ideally the system should be actually tested under such load conditions. Unfortunately this is usually not practical and consequently systems may be bought on the basis of "flashy" features rather than on the basis of performance and their ability to satisfy future as well as present needs.

On the basis of experience, I can assure you that bad response time will jeopardize any system. Concern about response time is one of the reasons we at NUL have delayed so long in implementing subject access. Bringing up a subject access system is not difficult; bringing up efficient subject access *is* difficult. The problem is that, unlike names, where the number of works under most headings is relatively small, there may be hundreds and hundreds of entries under a single subject heading. The processing load to manipulate the indexes and retrieve large numbers of records scattered all over the file is not trivial even on a mainframe.

DETERMINING USER NEEDS

Not only does the patron need fast response time, but the patron has other needs that should be taken into account, needs that card catalogs have never adequately met. Everyone recognizes the defects of the card catalog, but herein lies a real danger. There is a growing voice in the library community that says since the catalog is so inadequate why imitate it in the online catalog? Why not use the keyword, Boolean logic technique employed by the information retrieval services to provide access to indexing and abstracting databases? But beware! The content of a cataloging database is not the same as an indexing and abstracting database. Catalog data is highly structured, but the level of analysis is very low. The structure is its strength. We must not lose that strength until we are absolutely sure that there are compensations in the form of improved access. I am not convinced that, by itself, keyword access is a viable alternative to access via conventionally ordered browseable entries under consistently formulated headings. Consistency of headings in a card catalog ensures that a user, having found one entry under a heading, has found them all. I worry that comprehensiveness of recall will be sacrificed in a system which is completely keyword oriented.

Consistency in headings is obviously difficult to achieve in an indexing and abstracting database. Consequently, it is usually compensated for by providing additional access points. Consistency in headings is essential to an effective online catalog. Such consistency can only be achieved through a system which provides authority control and which has a syndetic structure which enables the user to approach the file by means of alternate forms of headings (i.e., cross references).

Another disadvantage of keyword access is that it assumes a level of user sophistication which, at least at present, may not be realistic. As reference people involved in searching indexing and abstracting databases know, some knowledge of the structure and content of the database is essential for successful searching. Can we be sure our users will understand the content and structure of a cataloging database?

Knowing how much trouble users of a card catalog have with corporate and conference headings (which abound in serial records), it is intriguing to think about keyword access for these materials. But consider, isn't it also true that many such names and many serial titles are made up solely of nondistinctive words, words which may occur hundreds and even thousands of times in a large database. Under such conditions, Boolean logic has to be very intelligently applied or else it will place an intolerable load on even a large mainframe computer.

In an attempt to cope with nondistinctive words, some systems set up "stop words" to keep the number of matches manageable. I cannot buy this approach. What is required is some type of positional or adjacency capabilities — "Medical" after "American" and before "Association." So now you are part way back to the concept of headings and references to those headings, the principles on which the catalog is based.

Obviously, the optimum arrangement is an online catalog which provides both keyword and locially ordered, contextual, heading-oriented access. Here the ogre of cost raises its head. Can you afford to have both access methods? At Northwestern we have some doubts. Until it is proved both that keyword access is truly effective, and until we can be sure we can support the cost of both types of access, we have elected to stay with our tested alphabetically ordered, contextual, pre-coordinated, and generically searchable indexes. Our rationale is that such indexes, if well supplemented with cross references, will serve most of our patrons most of the time at the least possible cost. For that small percentage of our users who require keyword access (for conference entries for example), we can always transfer them to the RLIN system which will contain a copy of our catalog.

Because we are depending on copious references to compensate for lack of keyword access, it is important that we have an online authority file. With such a file we can create all the references we have always wanted to have but never could produce in a manual catalog.

In addition to references, another feature which compensates for lack of keyword access in NOTIS is "browseability." If we analyze the mental process involved in browsing through a list of entries in a book catalog or a telephone directory, we see that a search can be begun at a very general level. Words in context are used to qualify and narrow a search. NOTIS indexes are designed to facilitate qualification in context. In effect they supply a sort of machine-assisted qualification, which eliminates the need for explicit qualification of the kind required in Boolean searching. The user of LUIS can enter the system using as a search term as little as the first word of a heading. The system then replies with an alphabetically ordered list of brief entries whose headings begin with that search term. The list is displayed in one or more "pages" of up to seventeen entries per page. Scanning through the entries, the user searches for words which trigger recognition. The process goes very fast, much faster than leafing through cards in a card catalog. Best of all, the process is simple and the concept is familiar.

From a machine standpoint, it is also very efficient. The secret lies in carrying the indexes in very large "blocks," with a high level of data compression. Each entry is "pre-coordinated," consisting of a heading followed by those data elements which, on the basis of experience, have been determined to be most useful in distinguishing one work from another. For example, a name record in the index contains part of the title, and conversely a title record will contain all or part of the main entry. If the index record is from a serial record, the place of publication is included in the index record; if a book, the date of publication is included.

By carrying the index entries in compressed form in large blocks in the same order as they will be displayed, and because a desired item can usually be identified at the index level, the number of file accesses necessary to satisfy a search is greatly reduced. By keeping the size of these entries to a minimum and by displaying them seventeen at a time, the amount of data which must be sent over communication lines is also kept to a minimum.

Another technique is used to assist the user who is vague about the form or spelling of a heading and consequently must use a nondistinctive search term which retrieves a large number of index entries. In such cases the system provides a "guide screen" from which the user can narrow the group of index entries to be examined. This guide screen consists of up to seventeen truncated index entries selected from all the entries retrieved by the search. An entry is selected or not selected for display as a guide term based on the degree to which it differs from previous entries. This prevents a guide term separating groups of very similar entries.

At present no index entry exceeds seventy-two characters. One of our planned refinements is to increase the maximum size of a heading to 120 characters. Not only will this avoid split files (where the works of two authors interfile because the last part of the heading had to be truncated), but it also will permit headings in the index entries to be used for authority control. Corporate and conference headings are most in need of this. Lengthening the maximum size will, of course, reduce the number of entries which can be displayed on a screen, but we hope to compensate for this by subarranging data which qualifies a heading under a single occurrence of the heading.

Regardless of whether access is by post-coordinated keyword indexes or by pre-coordinated contextual indexes, the real deficiency with catalog access is lack of analysis. One problem in searching any database by any means is that access points exist, but the user cannot find them. The other is that there are not adequate access points in the record. We desperately need what some people are calling "enriched cataloging." This could take the form of PRECIS, or it could involve the incorporation of tables of contents and indexes. Although indiscriminate keyword indexing is not appropriate, flagging of selective phrases in titles and notes in order to generate index entries should be considered, as should the increased use of "catch titles" and "augmented titles."

This brings up another issue — the use of title keywords for subject searching. Some believe that the "title" of a work invariably contains subject descriptors which are valuable for retrieval. This may be so for works in science and technology; it is not so true for works in other areas. If we count on accessing a catalog database through title keywords, we can expect to retrieve a large amount of nonrelevant materials, but even more seriously, much will be missed. What is a much better solution is for more and better subject headings to be assigned.

For serials and sets, but also for many single volume books, there is another way in which access could be greatly improved and that is by the increased use of analytics. At the Library of Congress, there has been developed a draft analytics format which needs to be finalized so it can be used and tested. At Northwestern we are using a version of this draft format to develop a file of analytic records for Africana conference papers. We are also using it for indexing data for journal articles in the transportation field. Our experience so far is very positive. We are using a technique whereby a record for the containing item is set up only once, with

111

automatic linking to the record for the analyzed item. Following the display of the analyzed item, the system retrieves and displays data from the containing item.

Another aspect of access is the provision of references. We need to provide more and better cross references for names, for subjects, and for series. At Northwestern, we have most of our name authority file in machine-readable form in the MARC authority format, and we are now in the process of converting our series authority records. Index records, derived from "see from" and "see also from" fields in authority records, will be incorporated in our indexes so that the proper "see" and "see also" references can be generated.

Another aspect of patron access is comprehensiveness and timeliness of the database. The optimum system must be able to inform the user not just about cataloged materials, but also about materials which have not yet been cataloged and even about materials which have not yet been received. Because the NOTIS database includes order and receipt records, LUIS is able to tell patrons that an item is on order or in process. For serials, the users are able to ascertain exactly what bound volumes are held and where they are located, exactly what current unbound issues are held and where they are located, and whether or not those holdings are available for use. The card catalog has never been able to provide this type of information. Users of LUIS have this information at their fingertips.

SERIALS HOLDINGS

What is the format of holdings information for serials? Back in 1974, as a member of the working group which eventually resulted in the CONSER project, I argued to no avail that work should be begun on a standard notation format for detailed serial holdings. The timing was not right. Most librarians were still thinking about printed union lists with summary holdings. No one visualized that online check-in systems could ever be integrated with online union catalogs and online interlibrary loan systems, all of which either require or benefit from detailed holding information. Belated as it is, there is now an ANSI committee charged with developing a standard for detailed holdings.

Because there was no standard, Northwestern had to develop its own format for detailed serials holdings. We hope that it will not be too incompatible with the eventual standard. We do know that our format has stood the test of time and use quite well. It is very human-readable, as well as concise. Although it is not as machine-manipulatable as I would like, we have tried to use conventions and an order of data elements which would be amenable to format recognition techniques. An unbroken run of thirty volumes, all volumes bound individually, would be expressed as follows:

v.1-30(1951-1980)

An example of a statement for the first ten issues of a serial published twelve times a year would be:

v.13,no.1-10(1980,jan-oct)

Of course there are many more complicated patterns which must be accommodated.

What is the patron's view of holdings information? When a serial volume is "added" to the collection, the cataloger or bindery staff member updates the volume holdings record. If a bound volume was constructed from loose periodical issues, the corresponding loose issue receipt statement in the order record is simultaneously deleted. All special issues (indexes, supplements, etc.) are reflected in the record. A convention has been developed to handle multiple series. Whenever a patron calls up a bibliographic record, these "bound volume" holdings are displayed immediately following the call number and location.

In addition, if a record for a periodical is displayed, the system extracts from the order record any receipt statements for current unbound issues and displays this data immediately following the information on bound volumes.

The net effect, for both books and serials, is that the patron knows the status and location of every item, whether bound or unbound, whether on order, in process, or cataloged, and whether it is in the stacks, in the reference room, in the periodical room, or in a mixture of locations (bound volumes in stacks; current volume or loose issues in the reference room or periodical room.)

AVAILABILITY INFORMATION

A maximally effective system should contain information not just about the existence of copies, volumes, and issues, but also about the availability of those copies, volumes, and issues. For a number of years Northwestern patrons have been able to directly inquire in our circulation files to determine if an item was already charged out. If the item is charged to an individual, the system only tells the patron that it is charged out and when it is due and informs him that he may request that it be called in. If the item is charged out to a "library function" (bindery, reserve room, lost or missing) or is out to a carrel, this information is conveyed to him so he does not have to make a fruitless trip to the stacks.

At present, the interconnection between our circulation and bibliographic systems is rather cumbersome. The user, finding a bibliographic record, writes down the call number, calls up the circulation access screen, and then keys in the call number. We have plans to make this interconnection automatic.

Good inventory control also contributes to user satisfaction with an online catalog. At present we maintain an inventory file on tape. It consists of one record for each physical piece in the collection. It is skeletal, containing only the location, call number, volume number, and copy number. Eventually we intend to load it into an online file to serve as a call number index to the bibliographic and holdings records. In the meantime it is very valuable for use in taking inventory, an activity which is conducted on an ongoing basis.

Inquiry into circulation files is simple. The patron simply types in the first two lines of the call number, and the system retrieves the records of all editions, copies, and volumes with that base call number which are not in their assigned location.

BIBLIOGRAPHIC DATA

Another consideration in designing a patron access system is how much bibliographic information to provide. Our experience is that brief information will serve most users most of the time, but that full bibliographic data needs to be available as an option. At present, as the default condition, LUIS displays only main entry, title, edition, imprint, series, and detailed holdings. For serials, we have plans to add any linking entry notes to the brief display to minimize the confusion caused by successive entry cataloging. We are now developing programs by which the full bibliographic record, in catalog-card-like form, can be displayed, but we hope that this will not be necessary for most users, since the editing and formatting of the data is processing intensive and requires that additional data be transmitted over the communications lines.

This brings up a very important point. With disk storage costs dropping so rapidly, libraries shouldn't even consider an online catalog which carries less than full bibliographic data. As recently as a few years ago, people were still talking seriously about having a subset of the full bibliographic data locally and using the bibliographic utility database if the full record was needed. This would either be very awkward for the user or else a very complex system linkage would be necessary. We are now at the point that if a library can afford an online catalog at all, it can afford the storage costs for the full bibliographic record.

THE USER INTERFACE

Another aspect of the online catalog is how the patron communicates with the system. This part of our system design has been a real challenge, primarily because there are so few systems which we could use as models. We pirated every good idea we could find, but there weren't many to choose from. We did learn some things from Ohio State University about the way their command language was structured. Since their indexes were similar to ours, their experience with patron access to those indexes was reassuring. We got the idea for our guide record technique from the Library of Congress system, although we modified it considerably. Unfortunately most other available systems (BRS, SDC, Lockheed, WLN, UTLAS, RLIN) were not of much use to us because our indexes didn't resemble theirs and because we did not want to go the keyword/Boolean logic route. As for user prompting, although we knew that some systems were being designed which provided elaborate "hand-holding" to help the user, we felt that the logic of our indexes was so simple that such hand-holding was unnecessary. We were also concerned about the extra processing load involved in the one-step-at-a-time approach. We were also concerned that the users, having learned how to use the system, would find a system designed for the novice too constraining, and we did not want to design one system for the inexperienced user and one for the experienced.

Our final decision was to use a simple command driven interface. Each screen has a list of one character commands which are valid for that screen. Each screen has a single "prompting" line which tries to anticipate the most logical next step; however, the user can elect to follow that prompting or not as he chooses. There are a minimum number of commands. An "a=" followed by all or part of a name will initiate an author search. A "t=" followed by a word or two from the title will cause a search by title. Line numbers are used with the guide and index screens to select a guide interval or call in a bibliographic record. From an index screen, the command "m" will cause the next page of index records to be displayed. From a bibliographic screen, the command "m" causes the next bibliographic record in sequence to be displayed. An "i" takes the user from a bibliographic record back to the index screen. A "g" takes the user from a bibliographic or index display back to the guide display. An "e" returns the user to the introductory screen. The introductory screen gives basic instructions for formulating a search. Each of the various other display screens (guide, index, and bibliographic) is backed up by a "help" screen which the user can call in by typing "?".

Perhaps the most common problem experienced by users is in formulating a search term. There is a tendency at first to use too explicit a search term (all of the author or title rather than just a word or two). Because the user often cannot predict the exact form of the name or title, the patron often gets back a "no entries found" message. In order to alleviate this problem, the text of this message has been expanded to instruct the user to call in the help screen to determine possible reasons for the unsuccessful search. This help screen clues the user in to alternative ways of finding the desired item, such as shortening the search term, checking for typos, etc.

The system is as "forgiving" of errors as possible. Before a search is conducted, the search term is "normalized" by setting it all to upper case, stripping out punctuation characters, removing excess blanks, etc. When a user has determined that a desired item exists, he can switch to the circulation inquiry screen by typing the command "d." This screen contains complete instructions for entering a call number and doing a circulation search.

Although the system is essentially self-instructing, we have also started to develop a more complete written manual of operation which will be available at each terminal. However, because we plan to make the system available from various nonlibrary sites, we are quite anxious that the user have access to adequate instructions online.

What really becomes obvious when you implement an online catalog is that users do not know how to use any catalog, card or online, effectively. We now have the opportunity to do a more effective job of providing bibliographic instruction. At Northwestern we feel we have made a start; much remains to be done.

PLANNED REFINEMENTS

We have many other improvements planned — some of them major, some minor. Most of the improvements which we must complete between now and January 1981 are relatively minor, but there are two major improvements which must be made by that time. One is the change in the index entries to allow more precise collocation of entries, to permit authority control, and to be able to supply cross references. The other refinement is the provision of subject access. Subject access was postponed not because our existing software and index structure could not be used, but because we were concerned that the processing requirements for retrieving large numbers of bibliographic records from the file would affect response time. The technique we plan to implement to keep performance high involves a modification of our index structure.

Instead of the single-tiered index which we use for author and title access, we plan a two-tiered subject index. The first level index will consist of records which only contain subject headings. There will be one record for each subject heading used plus an entry for each see from heading. As displayed, they will resemble a multi-paged subject-heading thesaurus. Like other indexes, the subject-heading index can be accessed by using all or part of the heading, and each screen will hold up to seventeen subject headings with their available subdivisions. These can be scanned and paged to find the most appropriate heading.

Unlike the author/title and title/author indexes, which are qualified with sufficient bibliographic data to permit the user to identify the exact work wanted before calling in the bibliographic record, information about the works under a subject heading will be carried in a second level index. This second level index will consist of very brief bibliographic records (title, date or place of imprint, location, and call number.). These brief records will be displayed in pages of up to seventeen entries to a screen. Experimentally, we plan to order books in reverse chronological order to test the theory that subject searchers prefer recent imprints over older materials. Serials will be ordered at the beginning of the list.

We anticipate that most patrons using the subject catalog will find this abbreviated information adequate without having to call in the full bibliographic record. This will lessen the processing load considerably since the abbreviated bibliographic records, like other indexes, are combined and compressed into large blocks.

117

On the list of projects we have in mind over the long term is to load the machine-readable LC subject heading file to provide a level of cross references never possible in the card catalog. Unfortunately, this project must wait until LC has worked out a viable method of distributing subject authority records.

Another change to the indexes is an increase in the maximum number of characters in headings. We have done some research on our database which indicates that if we set a maximum size at 120, we will be able to accommodate all but about 0.3 percent of headings. These are almost exclusively name/title headings, and in only a small fraction of these do the characters which make them unique fall after the 120th character. Lengthening the indexes will allow us to carry birth dates and qualifiers necessary to ensure proper collocation. More importantly, it will allow us to cope with government and other multi-divisioned corporate bodies more effectively.

CONCLUSION

At Northwestern we feel we have made a good start toward an online catalog; much remains to be done. We recognize that design of the perfect system is an evolutionary process, and first-generation systems will be flawed. The best one can hope for is that the foundation was properly laid so the flaws will not be fatal. In the meantime our guiding principle will continue to be to bring up a prototype system, make it available for use, observe it in use, then go back and modify the system. This iterative process is the only practical and effective way to arrive at the optimum system.

Our experience so far indicates that an online catalog is a reasonable and desirable alternative to the card catalog. After thirteen years devoted to developing NOTIS to the point where it can perform almost all the behind-the-scenes library functions more efficiently, NOTIS, with a face-lift and using the alias LUIS, has emerged from the backroom into the public eye.

DISCUSSION

Kaye Gapen, Iowa State University: When you tested the system, did you see anything in the serials holding format that you would have changed as people used it?

Ms. Veneziano: We did our serials conversion in 1970 and had no choice but to use what was on the shelflist. At that point, we used some cryptic abbreviations which in retrospect I would have preferred not to have had in the serials holding statement. We are gradually identifying these and weeding them out, and so far I think our serials holdings format has not been a problem for the patron.

Bob Houbeck, University of Michigan: In experimenting with faculty acceptance of using terminals, did you consider putting terminals in the offices of departments that are more local on campus so that those people could use them more and get used to them? Secondly, how do you determine how many terminals your library community needs and where you put them?

Ms. Veneziano: I think there is no doubt that faculty members are reluctant to come up to a bank of public terminals, sit down with students who have been using terminals since high school, and start trying to figure it all out. So yes, we do plan to put terminals in faculty offices so that they can experiment in private. As to how many terminals, we don't know. Before we installed the patron use terminals, we did some studies in which we compared the time it takes to do searching on the terminals with the searches performed at the card catalog. The number of terminals which would be required turned out to be very low; I feel we can't rely on this type of study and may have to triple our original estimates. However, it is not the cost of terminals which I worry about since these are now relatively inexpensive. What we are concerned about is having enough computer power to handle the large number of searches which we anticipate when we make terminals widely available.

The Future of Serials Control
and Its Administrative Implications
for Libraries

MICHAEL GORMAN

Increasingly, my library philosophy could be summed up as one of creative unbelief. I find as one gets older and more involved in administration, one finds it difficult to believe readily and can use that unbelief to challenge accepted ideas and to find solutions. My unbelief extends to the necessity for the existence of serials. I believe that serials are an expensive and inefficient form of communication, and that they are a major factor in the decline in the quality and integrity of the collections in our large libraries. Further, I believe that we, as librarians, have to face the fact that we should play a part in finding a new and better form of communication.

Realistically, in the short term I recognize that serial publications are a major factor in the library economy and that we have to address the problems they pose with the application of modern techniques. A key element in library administration is the belief that changes in techniques are, and should be recognized to be, closely related to changes in administration, in administrative philosophy, and in the broader philosophy of our profession. In particular, what happens to serials (now and in the future) requires a reconsideration of the manner in which we run parts of our libraries, the manner in which we run entire libraries, and the various ways in which libraries interact with each other.

Before addressing my main topic, I wish to expand on the reasons behind my belief that serials should be done away with and

Michael Gorman is director of the Technical Services Department of the University of Illinois Library that librarians should contribute to the reformation of the whole structure of serial publishing. Broadly, there are two reasons. The first is economic, and the second is related to the inefficiency of serials as a means of communication.

As far as the economics are concerned, there can be no doubt that the cost of purchasing, maintaining, binding, and storing serials is seriously attacking the integrity of our major library collections. This phenomenon is especially marked in the areas of the sciences and social sciences. We are dealing with increases in the costs of acquiring serials which approach 20 percent for domestic titles and often approach 30 percent for foreign titles. One must remember that these serial acquisitions represent continuing commitments and that the rate of increase shows no sign of decreasing. That is, once one's library is committed to buying a particular serial title, one will have to live with that 20-30 percent increase every year. The processes of checking and claiming serial titles grow more baroque and more expensive with the passing of each year. The current rate for the binding of serial volumes, for most libraries, is in excess of eight dollars a volume. Looking at the budgets of large libraries, one can see that the inevitable consequences are already occurring. Libraries are having to do one or both of the following: cancellation of serials or the transfer of money from monograph to serial budgets. Most libraries which have endured a serial cancellation project will do almost anything to avoid a repetition of the experience. The other possibility is to switch money from one area of the materials budget to another and to switch staff and other resources from monograph to serials processing. This switching of resources is irreversible without a serials cancellation project.

All this expense and grief and erosion of monographic acquisitions is dedicated to the acquiring and storing of objects which per item and per title are very little used. Anyone who studies the use of library collections and, in particular, the work of Bradford and followers, will be aware that relatively few serial titles account for the overwhelming majority of the use of the total collection of serials.[1] This means, obviously, that a great many serial titles have small use, and that that use often approaches zero. It has been estimated that the average journal article is read by fifteen persons. This means that, if one takes into account the articles that are read by a large number of persons, there are many articles which may be read by the author and his or her friends and relations, if they are read at all.

121

Among other practical reasons for my belief that we should find another means of communication are, first, that there are far too many journals. No one can keep up with all the journals in a field, even if that field is relatively specialized. Second, many of these countless journals are published for the wrong reasons. We all know, even in our own civilized and high-minded field, of journals which exist to satisfy the vanity of the editor and of journals which exist, by and large, to aid the tenure process in academic libraries. Third, these numerous serials are next to impossible to control bibliographically. Most libraries do not claim all their outstanding serials because their systems do not give them information on missing journal issues until it is too late. With a certain amount of exaggeration, one could hypothesize that paper-based serials control systems in libraries have no positive effect whatever. It would be interesting to find and study a library brave enough to abandon its paper-based serial control system. It is likely that that library would receive the journals that it was receiving anyway and would not receive the journals that it was not receiving. Meanwhile, it would be saving an enormous amount of money, mostly in staff time. My recent administrative experience, with paper-based serial systems control in particular, has led me to a theory which is probably not entirely new: probably the only way to do efficient claiming is to claim everything. Under such a system one would send out a claim regularly for every serial one takes. The notice would bear a disclaimer saying "If this item has already been sent, disregard this notice." This would be a relatively inexpensive and effective system.

The truth is that librarians cannot control serials, and that indexing and abstracting services cannot control serials, and that library users themselves cannot control serials. We are suffering not from an "information explosion" but from a "printed serials explosion."

Are monographs, then, inherently better than serials? I would answer yes. I believe that serials are a filtration device for knowledge, ideas, and information. Those ideas, knowledge, and information which are valuable will find their way eventually into monographs. The vast majority of bad, meretricious, temporary, or ephemeral ideas and information appearing in serials will remain unread and expensively bound in crowded library stacks.

The solution to all of this, in my opinion, is that we should employ a well established technique — the selective dissemination of information. Using that technique we would match individual articles with individual and library profiles and, thereby, supply individuals and libraries with "tailor-made" journals. Individual articles would, when accepted following a neutral refereeing process, be stored in computerized clearinghouses. They could be disseminated in microform, on paper, or by electronic transfer. The economics of the system would be based on individual and corporate subscriptions to the services provided by the clearinghouses. Librarians need to work with publishers, with authors, with indexing and abstracting services, and with all other interested parties to solve the problems that serials pose for all of us.

Meanwhile, how do we cope with the serial now? There are two general approaches for us to take. First, we need new and creative ideas about serial control. Second, we need automated, online, decentralized, integrated systems for serials control. In considering the first approach, we do well to remember that the key injunction of Charles Ammi Cutter, the great prophet of our profession, has been ignored in serials control. He said, *apropos* of cataloging, that the convenience of the user should never be sacrificed to the convenience of the librarian. In our techniques of serial control, we have largely ignored the convenience of the user in order to suit the convenience of librarians and the administrative structure in which they work. For example, cataloging rules rarely address the real problems of serial control. There are no cataloging rules that tell one how to record serial holdings. No cataloging rules define in unambiguous and practical terms what a serial is. A matter bedeviling union catalogs and cooperative databases is the fact that two librarians, using an identical set of cataloging rules, can catalog two copies of the same item completely differently. Each of them is, in his or her light, correct. One will treat the item as a monographic serial. Another will treat the item as a monograph within a series. Unfortunately, the resulting records bear no relation to each other. The reason for this confusion is that cataloging rules do not deal with the first and most important decision — what is it that one is cataloging?

Another example of the failure of standards for serial control is demonstrated by the fact that serial control systems generally deal with serials at the highest and least useful level. This approach is typified by cataloging at the level of the monographic series, or, even worse, that aberrant version of the monographic series, the made-up series. An example of the difficulties caused by this approach is the single entry for a series of conferences. Each publication has its own title, editor, subject, date of publication, etc.

Unfortunately, one cannot find an individual work by any of these characteristics because they are hidden in the catalog under a catch-all heading such as "Conferences on High Energy Physics. Proceedings, Vol. 1—." Considering the way in which people use serial information, it seems obvious that they are much more interested in information at more specific levels. To use Ranganathan's terminology, the focus of interest is at the level of micro-thought — the individual article or the individual volume within a monographic series. There is no doubt that if serial control concentrated more on indexing (that is, providing records for the individual articles) and on analytical cataloging (that is, providing records for individual volumes), library users would be much better served.

Another difference I would like to see in our approach to serial control is more interaction between librarians and serial publishers. For example, a simple solution to a perennial problem would be to arrange for every issue of a serial to carry a bar code containing the International Standard Serial Number (ISSN) and data indicating the volume and the issue number. This would lead to the speedy automatic check-in of serials. It would cost the publishers very little indeed. I am sure the only reason why they have not embarked on such a scheme is because nobody has asked them.

In summary, we need a revolution in our thinking about serial control, lending a more reader-oriented approach which takes into account the use of serials rather than the easiest way of dealing with them.

We also need the kind of automated, online, decentralized, integrated systems which have been foreshadowed in the previous papers of this conference. "Decentralized" is an important adjective. One needs to have the ability to check serials in at their point of use. A common pattern of serial check-in in large libraries is for the library to maintain a centralized check-in system and to send each issue of each serial to departmental or branch libraries, each of which maintains a duplicate check-in system staffed by clerical workers. It should be possible to get rid of one of the two check-in systems. It is unlikely that one can eliminate the second; therefore, one must give the power of check-in to the individual units within the library. That in itself will speed up the processing because individual issues can be delivered directly to the departmental or branch libraries. Once received, the issues will be checked in on a terminal, and the receipt registered in a centralized database.

Another attribute of future serial control systems is that they will be "integrated." I have believed for all of the twelve years or so that I have been interested in library automation that we should have integrated systems. Check-in (as should all other activities) should form part of a continuum. The library should have a single system which answers questions of ownership, circulation, ordering, binding, etc., with one referral. Recently, I have begun to question that idea a little. Listening to the paper on the NLM experience and listening to the ideas of commercial vendors, I begin to wonder whether integrated systems are entirely desirable. They are certainly very attractive conceptually. However, some way of dealing with serials which is self-contained could conceivably be more efficient and less expensive. It has been suggested that effective automated serials control can only be achieved by designing a dedicated terminal only for serial check-in and claiming which has no relation to the other parts of your automated system. Such suggestions add to the uncertainty which is building around the concept of integrated automated systems.

The problems of achieving online serial systems, whether integrated or not, essentially revolve around human and financial resources. In other words, we all know that the systems are desirable, but who is going to design them and how are we going to pay for them? There are two ways in which one should approach those questions. (Incidentally, I believe that there is another problem which has not been mentioned — the psychological problems. We achieved automated circulation systems relatively easily because we were psychologically ready for them. The kind of iron that enters into one's soul after a lifetime of dealing with serials makes one psychologically unready for progressive solutions!) One approach is to look at the staff savings which will undoubtedly result from the achievement of automated serials systems. Paper systems are labor-intensive in the worst possible way. They consume an enormous amount of time and supply the people who carry out the task with a job that is at best barely endurable. We should plan, therefore, for a considerable reduction in staff to help pay for a more cost-effective online system. Second, we must consider the way in which the future systems will be financed. I believe that they will be financed at the state or regional level. If one looks at the progress in automated library systems, in areas other than serial control, one can see that a well organized and energetic state system can achieve a great deal. Also, much can be achieved regionally by means of consortia or networks. An alternative lies in the use of commercial concerns. Such use will depend upon a symbiotic relationship in which the vendors' interest lies in setting up a system which will benefit the library as well as benefitting themselves commercially.

There are two solutions which I find intensely unattractive. One is that of the individual library devising its own system. This is not to say that individual systems which have been achieved thus far are necessarily bad; it is to say that any library starting now with the idea of achieving an online serial control system should not go it alone. At best one could only achieve (at great expense) an inward looking system which would not benefit other libraries and other library users in a community, state, and region. The other idea that I find unattractive is that of a national serial control system. It is impossible to devise a national system which will suit the great variety of libraries which would be its participants. If one looks at the history of American library automation (for example, the tremendous success of OCLC), one sees a spreading out of systems from the bottom rather than systems being imposed on the local level from on high. I believe that there is something in the American library psychology which demands an expanding local system rather than an imposed national system.

To return to the implications for organization of libraries, I believe that present and future technological advances are going to have implications which are difficult for most of us to foresee. Normally, what happens when someone invents a better mousetrap is that one has the same house, only one which contains a better mousetrap. In libraries, however, it is a mistake to achieve a technological advance and then to try to run the library as usual with the only difference being a slightly improved process.

I believe that there are three steps which we should take in reforming the processes and the structure of libraries and the ways in which libraries interact. These are progressive steps given here in the order in which they should occur.

First, we should organize technical processing by function and not by form. That is, instead of having a department which deals with a particular kind of material (serials, continuations, monographs, etc.), we should have departments or divisions which deal with ordering, with claiming and receiving, with cataloging, with binding, and so on, irrespective of the nature of the materials. The overriding reason for this suggestion is that organization by form inevitably leads to a dislocation, leading to pointless differences in the treatment of materials. If one has two groups of people — one called the serials acquisitions department and the other called the monograph acquisitions department — inevitably they are going to be carrying out processes in a slightly different manner despite the fact that the different materials often do not call for different treatment. Because there is no satisfactory standard definition of a serial, the items in the serials department and the items in the monographs department may be very similar but be treated differently.

For example, in some libraries the serials department includes a documents division. If, as stated in an earlier paper, the only true definition of a serial is an item dealt with by the serials department, then in such a library all documents are serials. Since all one needs to establish a serial is a number, and since a document without a number is as rare as a doctor without a BMW, one can make a case for all documents being serials. The point is that many of the documents in such a library are processed as serials to the detriment of the user. The user cannot find them because the user is thinking of an individual report (again, the lower level of the bibliographic hierarchy) and cannot fit that into the complex structure imposed on government serials. If we organize by function, we will have a more consistent treatment of materials to the benefit of the library user.

Second, we should abolish the split between technical services and public services. The decentralized check-in and decentralized cataloging which would be available to us for serials will help in this endeavor and enable us to achieve the following structure in our libraries.

I believe that libraries in the future will contain three kinds of groups of librarians and other staff. First, there will be a central, automated, clerically staffed processing unit. This unit will place orders, maintain the automated records of claiming, cataloging, binding, etc. It will contain a relatively small number of people. No professional librarians will be involved in the day-to-day operation of the unit. Second, there will be an administrative segment dealing with personnel matters, budget matters, planning matters, and so on. Third, and most important, there will be groups of librarians and support staff organized around various subject or service categories. This group will include, for example, a group of science librarians, a group of literature librarians, a group giving undergraduate services, a group giving children's services, groups concerned with the librarianship of area and language studies (such as Slavic librarians, Africana librarians, and Asian librarians). The professionals in these groups will carry out all the professional activities connected with their subject or service. They will select materials, do original cataloging, give reader service, do bibliographic instruction, etc. The activities will all take place in contact with the automated and decentralized system. Such an organization will achieve a more rounded approach to the profession of librarianship in which professionals become complete librarians again. Even more importantly, it will achieve better reader service. The worst thing about the technical services/public services division has been that it has deprived the users of contact with some very fine librarians. Many of our technical services librarians know an enormous amount about the materials they process, and yet they are seldom called upon to communicate that information to the users of the library.

Third, we should abolish separate libraries. Having integrated everything within the individual libraries and having linked those libraries by automated resource sharing systems, we will have achieved, by one means or another, large "electronic libraries." In these electronic libraries a person in any part of the state or regional system will have the ability to find bibliographic information and to request desired items. Obviously, for some time we are going to have separate university libraries, separate college libraries, separate public libraries, separate special libraries, which to all intents and purposes will have become storage places, reading rooms, etc. The real library will be the electronic library because the most important thing about a library is not its architecture or its physical plant or even, to a certain extent, its individual reader service, but its ability to find materials that you want to use. If one can sit at a computer terminal in Coal Valley, Illinois, and scan the resources of the University of Illinois at Urbana Library or the University of Wisconsin at Madison Library and, having found something which one wants, have it delivered, in essence one is a patron of those libraries.

We must begin to do something about a catastrophic situation. Paper serials control systems, particularly in large libraries, are a catastrophe. They are a waste of time, a waste of money, and a waste of human resources. If we begin by taking some of the steps outlined above we will end up with a system (the electronic library) which has enormous implications on the administration of libraries and on the philosophy of librarianship. We will end up, because of this kind of advance in technique, belonging to a rather different profession and doing rather different and more satisfying things.

128

REFERENCE

1. For a useful summary of these issues, see F. W. Lancaster's *Measurement and Evaluation of Library Services* (Washington, D.C.: Information Resources Press, 1977).

DISCUSSION

Richard Meyer, Clemson University: In regard to your concept of breaking up the library into units, say organized around subjects, how would you coordinate evenness of services and quality of services in that kind of structure?

Mr. Gorman: I think that you can use the machine to help you with that. One of the reasons you have a cataloging department is so you can have a head cataloger who can impose quality control. There is someone there to make sure the cataloging is being done properly, to instruct, to guide, to mold, etc. Now you can do that on a machine just as well as you can do it personally. So you have to build in quality control mechanisms which do not depend on physical proximity of the quality controller and the person doing the work. And so it seems to me that it is a problem whether you have a barnlike room full of people or whether there are people doing cataloging all over your campus or library. But the machine, I think, enables you to control it in the second instance just as well as the physical proximity enables you to control it in the first instance.

Incidentally, I think the major problem in achieving what I am talking about is not personal, psychological, or professional resistance, but the physical plant. I think it is going to be very difficult because our library buildings are built around certain concepts, including big cataloging rooms. How do you find a room for these distributed groups of librarians? I think this is going to be a big problem. I would hope that if we ever see any new library buildings that they will be built along that line. I think it would be a tragedy if someone was to put a lot of money into a big library building that would be based on old ideas.

Dan Tonkery, University of California, Los Angeles: I wondered in your three rules of organization if you considered organizing by personality rather than by function. But, you don't have to answer that.

129

Mr. Gorman: As a fellow director of technical services of a large research library, you are not supposed to disclose such secrets.

Mr. Tonkery: I have one other question. One of the pressures that you have as an administrator of technical services is deciding to what degree to involve faculty when you want to make changes. I don't know if you face a similar problem, but when you decide to make changes in an operating unit or an organizational component, one of the things to consider is that many of your people have long established ties with faculty members, and they are, if you will, going *sub rosa* saying an individual's idea is going to destroy the Hebrew collection or is going to destroy the Slavic material, or theatre arts. On a large campus there are multi-interest groups which are vocal only at the suggestion of change. How do you deal with the faculty component first, and how do you work around the employees to reinstill confidence?

Mr. Gorman: The answer is the same as to the question: "How do porcupines make love?" The answer is "With extreme difficulty." I think the only group in an academic library that is more resistant to change than the librarians is the teaching faculty. Mostly, those people are very interested in their use of the library in, essentially, beating the system. They have found a way of getting what they want. And they are not interested at all in the library as a whole, or the administration of the library, or structure of the library for they know a certain person who will always get the books that they need. It is very difficult and I think there are two things that you can do to ensure that, whatever the perception is, you never in fact diminish a service. You can always prove that the service is nòt being taken away. And the second thing is that by trying to maneuver your way around people who haven't been very effective, you are almost *ipso facto* encouraging other people to be as effective as they can be. It sounds very sanctimonious, but I am seriously proud of some of the people that we have in technical services in Illinois. They are very fine librarians, and I think to encourage the good people is the good side of having to discourage the people who aren't so good.

So I think that the way you work with the teaching faculty is to always maintain the service. You cannot do anything about the perception, but you can do something about the facts. And the way to deal with library communities is to find particular strengths which have been hidden. Because one of the things about poor administrative structures, and I think many of our libraries have poor administrative structures, is that essentially they grind down good people. They are machines for not bringing the best out of people, and if you can produce a new structure, you find you can bring the best out of people. I am sorry that did sound very pious. Now Kaye is going to tell us how it is really done.

Kaye Gapen, Iowa State University: Well, I just have a little question. In speaking closely with those few people from the University of Illinois who are allowed out, it does seem that even though areas and functions have been renamed there, nevertheless, people who did serials before continue to do serials now. I worked at Ohio State University where the idea of having tribes of librarians meet together in certain subject areas originated. "Tribes" is a very good simile because what happens with tribes is that you generally end up fighting it out at some point. At Ohio State, tribes of people met, and people were going to do both cataloging and reference work and serials and monographs. In fact, they divided things up and continued to specialize rather than becoming complete generalists. I wonder if you see this as a transition or something that is going to continue in the future?

Mr. Gorman: It seems to me that you can change the structure which will allow people to reorganize their working lives, but you cannot force people to do that. But if someone is trained as a serials cataloger and you put them in a general cataloging department, often they will carry on unless you absolutely force them not to do serials cataloging only. And this is what has happened to a certain extent at Illinois. But I think there are two positive features about that transitional phase. One is that even if you have, which we do not have incidentally, a group of serials catalogers and a group of monograph catalogers all within the same department, you have at least got some kind of integrated and consistent approach to cataloging. In other words, the department exists in that set-up to make sure that the anomalies which existed when you had completely separate serial and monograph cataloging departments do not exist.

The other thing, of course, is simply to use the turnover and changes in staffing to your advantage. I have learned in a very hard way both here and in setting up the British Library, which was a seismic event compared with which any changes at the University of Illinois are just little ripples, that one of the best things you can do is cultivate the sense of who can have their work patterns changed and who cannot. It will break your heart at any moment to try to change the unchangeable. Some people simply will never change their attitudes or their work habits. But you work on the ones that will, and as you bring in new people you introduce them to new concepts. It is a transitional thing, and it could take many years, depending on the turnover in your library. It is not quite as bad as you said. I think your implication was that there was still a strict division between serials and monographs right the way through technical services. It is really not like that at all. And if you think only tribes war together, you should look at the departments that existed before you set up the tribes.

Becky Lenzini, University of Illinois Library: What Michael says is true. We are still in a transition moving toward the integration of serials and monographs, but you can see the integration in full effect in some very definite areas. Not unreasonably, these areas are actually at the clerical end. For example, when there were separate serial and monograph cataloging units, monographs had a certain number of OCLC terminals and serials had their number of terminals. We now have nine terminals in one general area administered by one person, and we make sure they are used all day from eight in the morning until nine at night. The same people do monograph inputting and serial inputting. They are not specialists. At the lower level, I think we really have got a fair amount of integration of serials and monographs processing. I would be willing to expound on this to anybody in private.

Mr. Gorman: You are aided there by the fact that nonprofessional staff turnover is much greater than the professional staff.

Catherine Schell, Rochester Institute of Technology: One parting shot at Illinois. You mention Mickey Mouse procedures, and I will be the first to admit that this is true, but has your organization found a way to eliminate them yet?

Mr. Gorman: I think that we have eliminated a lot of things. Let me give you the first example which occurs to me. Up to less than three years ago, every single order placed by the University of Illinois was searched to an enormous extent. I mean it was searched through the *National Union Catalog, Books in Print,* all kinds of things. Hours and hours were spent on searching these orders, when in fact, at the time they arrived in the department where they were searched, they were perfectly reasonable orders which could have been placed and the items would have arrived in the library. The reason why this searching was being done was to establish the main entry. So, of course, the order file was in main entry order. There is no point in doing that. Half the time the main entries they established were wrong anyway. Because of dearly beloved superimposition, you never really knew when you found an entry in the National Union Catalog whether it was the right heading or not. And then when people were searching the order file for duplicates, they could never find them because they could not predict what the main entry was. So we changed that, with some difficulty, to a title file and cancelled most searching of orders and that has speeded up the process enormously. That is just one of a number of things. We have cut down on the number of paper files. Not to the extent to which I would like, but we cut out a great number of them.

Appendix

Descriptions of Automated Serials Control Systems

THE NATIONAL LIBRARY OF MEDICINE

In addition to the authoritative serials cataloging data available in CATLINE, its online catalog file, the National Library of Medicine currently maintains an automated serials processing system including approximately 42,000 serial titles. Although NLM still maintains manual check-in records for about 40 percent of the 22,000 serials currently received, all other aspects of serials control are managed by the manipulation of data in a network of files referred to as the MASTER SERIALS SYSTEM (MSS). The MSS consists of eight modules or files: (1) SERIALS (bibliographic data); (2) SUBSCRIP (subscription data); (3) JAF (indexing authority data); (4) GAPS (missing issues); (5) FILM (data on microfilmed issues); (6) BINDING (binding history and instructions); (7) CHECKIN; and (8) LOCATOR (location symbols for many U.S. medical libraries). Using a combination of elements from the eight files, NLM is able to produce subscription orders, backissue orders, binding pull slips, shelf markers, and four serial reference publications, among other products. The MSS serves in-house serial control needs and provides the basis for the SERLINE file, which is produced monthly for public access on NLM's online services network.

Written by Martha R. Fishel, the assistant head of the Serials Records Section of the National Library of Medicine, and Betsy L. Humphreys, chief of NLM's Technical Services Division.

Software

The MSS is operational under a database management system software called INQUIRE, which is a proprietary product of Infodata Systems, Inc. INQUIRE has extensive information retrieval, report generation, and database maintenance features which are accessible through an easy to use English-like user language. The INQUIRE user can call in any of the built-in services of the language or establish and store special prompt commands and display formats.

Each INQUIRE file consists of records which are composed of several information units (fields). Any number of fields can be indexed for easy retrieval, but regardless of whether they appear in an indexed field, all data in an INQUIRE file are accessible by sequential scan of all records in the file. INQUIRE also provides a means of relating logical records in different physical files, both in searching and in output. In the case of the MSS, a nine-digit control number is the link or the one common field contained in each of the eight files. Because different kinds of processing data are stored in different files and accessed and output together only as needed, record sizes and structures can be optimized and major modifications to any module of the system have little or no impact on the rest of the operation.

New records are added either directly online or are keypunched from data input forms and added weekly in a batch mode. Virtually all modifications to existing records are made online. Online maintenance allows the user to review input immediately and make any necessary corrections.

Overview of the Master Serials System Files

The MSS presently consists of the eight files described below.

1. The SERIALS file contains bibliographic information for all (approximately 42,000) titles in the MSS. All records in other MSS files must be linked to a specific SERIALS record. Records are carried for all serial titles or numbered congresses which are on order, in process, or currently received for the NLM collection. SERIALS also contains records for many ceased titles, for titles purchased for use by NLM staff, and for titles which have been withdrawn from the NLM collection. Additional ceased titles in the NLM collection are gradually being added to the MSS.

135

In addition to bibliographic elements such as title, publisher, first/last issue, subject headings, call number, etc., the SERIALS file carries data used to control the flow of new serial titles to cataloging (e.g., cataloger's initials, date sent to cataloging, series decision).

2. The SUBSCRIP file contains subscription information for all currently received serials and numbered congresses. Each unit record represents one order or subscription and is assigned a unique order number. The SUBSCRIP file carries information about the subscription, such as the source of procurement, number of copies, order date, beginning volume and year, as well as information about the disposition of the serial piece when it is received in the library (i.e., shelving and routing locations). Weekly orders are generated from the file in batch, incorporating some bibliographic data from SERIALS. Statistics and reports on serial ordering activity are produced from the SUBSCRIP file.

3. The BINDING file includes both the history of binding of a title at NLM as well as its current binding status. Each BINDING unit record represents one bound copy of one title. The BINDING file contains general binding instructions, such as when to bind, color, etc., and processing control information, such as when an item was pulled, date sent to the bindery, and date returned. Three-by-five binding pull slips and shelf charges are generated daily from the BINDING and SERIALS file. Instructions to the binder and summary statistics on the binding activity are also generated from this file.

4. The JAF (Journal Authority File) includes information necessary for control of MEDLARS journals in the indexing cycle. Two serial publications, the *List of Journals Indexed in Index Medicus* and the *List of Serials and Monographs Indexed for On-line Users* are pulled based on data in the JAF and SERIALS files. One record is carried for each title which is currently or was previously indexed for any MEDLARS bibliography (including *Index Medicus*) or for the MEDLINE, Health Planning and Administration, and POPLINE network retrieval files.

5. The GAPS file contains a description of specific serial issues which have been identified as missing from the NLM collection. Each GAPS record contains missing issue information for a single serial title. GAPS records are identified and entered into the file by serial records staff, circulation and control staff, or the NLM binding preparation contractor. A GAPS record carries specific year, volume, and issue information as well as fields to control systematic ordering and receipt of gap issues. The GAPS file is used to

alert NLM personnel and the public to the fact that some issues of serial runs are missing and not available at NLM.

6. The FILM file serves as a means of identifying those titles that have been purchased on microfilm or filmed at NLM for micropreservation purposes. A FILM record is entered for each title for which NLM holds microfilm. A FILM record includes specific year, volume, and issue information and a detailed description of when and why issues were pulled for filming, where they went, when they returned, and how many reels were returned per title.

7. The CHECKIN file is designed to contain current holdings and claim information for all serials and numbered congresses in the NLM collection. Currently, the file is used primarily as a repository for machine-readable data supplied by off-site check-in dealers. Issues currently received directly at NLM are not checked in online. About 60 percent of the 22,000 current subscriptions at NLM are received "off-site" and checked in by subscription agents who then supply NLM with monthly check-in tapes and weekly or twice weekly shipments with packing lists. Each CHECKIN record contains specific year, volume, issue and copy number information and indicates if the issue was sent or claimed with the date the action was taken.

8. The LOCATOR file was created for the purpose of identifying which U.S. medical school libraries owned significant biomedical serials in the NLM collection. Presently the file contains location symbols only for 120 libraries. In late 1981, the LOCATOR file will be replaced by a HOLDINGS data file.

In 1981 the MSS will be expanded to include an additional file for holdings and locator information for approximately 500 biomedical libraries from all eleven regions in NLM's Regional Medical Library Program. A HOLDINGS record will represent a library's holdings of one title. A holdings data format is currently being developed for online and union list display, based on the American National Standards Institute standard for summary holdings data. NLM will produce union lists beginning in the fall of 1981 when holdings information will appear in *Health Sciences Serials,* a microfiche publication produced by the Library.

SERLINE

SERLINE (SERials-onLINE) is the public version of NLM's Master Serials System and is regenerated monthly from the MSS. It contains approximately 35,000 bibliographic entries excluding withdrawn titles, out-of-scope titles, and NLM office copies. SERLINE includes elements from five of the eight files of the MSS. The SERLINE file was designed to assist in interlibrary loan and cooperative acquisitions activities throughout the Regional Medical Library Network. SERLINE is controlled by the ELHILL software at NLM and is searchable by a large variety of terms including textword, call number, main headings, title key, country, and almost every other bibliographic element. In addition, the user can request online or offline prints. Journal price information, NLM gaps, and resource library location symbols are all available to the SERLINE user.

Publications

Four serials reference publications are produced from data in the MSS. They are: (1) *Health Sciences Serials;* (2) *Index of NLM Serial Titles;* (3) *List of Journals Indexed in Index Medicus;* and (4) *List of Serials and Monographs Indexed for Online Users.* *Health Sciences Serials* is produced directly from the INQUIRE files; the other three publications are produced from SERLINE and use the computerized photocomposition capabilities of NLM's MEDLARS software.

Health Sciences Serials is a quarterly microfiche publication which includes approximately 35,000 serials and numbered congresses in the MSS which are on order, in process, currently or formerly received at NLM. Bibliographic, locator, and gap information are displayed. One noteworthy feature is that the visible header on each microfiche includes both the first and last titles which appear on that fiche.

The *Index of NLM Serial Titles* is an annual key-word-out-of-context (KWOC) index which also contains approximately 35,000 titles. The index is designed to assist librarians in the quick identification of biomedical serials and to provide the information needed to request serial interlibrary loans from NLM. The index is arranged so that each serial appears once for each keyword in the title. Certain generic words such as proceedings, journal, zeitschrift, etc., are not used as index terms. The index interfiles entries for both main title and added entries. All entries include the title and NLM call number, but only main entries are followed by the ISSN and the nine-digit NLM title control number.

The *List of Journals Indexed in Index Medicus* (LJI) is published in the January issue of *Index Medicus* and in the annual

Cumulated Index Medicus. In addition, *LJI* appears as a separate annual publication early each year. As of January, 1980, 2,630 journals were being indexed for *Index Medicus. LJI* is divided into four sections:

1. Alphabetical listing by abbreviated title followed by full title
2. Alphabetical listing by full title followed by abbreviated title
3. Listing by subject
4. Listing by country of origin.

For interlibrary loan purposes, the NLM call number appears at the end of each entry in *LJI* as well as the ISSN, if available.

New in 1980 was the first annual edition of the *List of Serials and Monographs Indexed for Online Users,* designed to provide complete bibliographic information on serials and monographs cited in three MEDLARS files: MEDLINE, Health Planning and Administration (called HEALTH), and POPLINE. Serials in HEALTH and POPLINE are indexed by outside institutions as a cooperative venture with NLM. Various subsets of the citations in these files are published in a variety of recurring bibliographies including *Index Medicus, Index to Dental Literature, International Nursing Index,* and *Hospital Literature Index.* The 1980 *List of Serials and Monographs Indexed for Online Users* contains 3,745 serial entries listed alphabetically by title abbreviation. Monographs are listed alphabetically by cataloging main entry.

Health Sciences Serials, Index of NLM Serial Titles, and the *List of Journals Indexed in Index Medicus* are all available from the Superintendent of Documents, U.S. Government Printing Office, Washington, D.C. The *List of Serials and Monographs Indexed for Online Users* is available from the National Technical Information Service in Springfield, Virginia.

NORTHWESTERN UNIVERSITY

NOTIS (Northwestern Online Total Integrated System) is a comprehensive library materials control system which supports all the major activities associated with acquiring materials, processing, managing, and cataloging them, and making them available to the public.

Technical Description

The system has two major components: circulation control and technical processing, each with two "aspects" — staff and patron. Each component includes online (real time) programs and offline (batch) programs. The online programs are used for the creation and update of records; the offline programs are used for the preparation of various types of reports (e.g., fine and overdue notices, catalog cards, purchase orders, customized correspondence, cataloging worksheets, etc.). There are also offline programs for various file maintenance operations and to maintain a file of Library of Congress catalog records.

The online programs operate under the control of the IBM teleprocessing monitor CICS/VS. The part of the system which creates and updates bibliographic, holdings, and order records consists of about eighteen programs, averaging about 3,000 bytes in size. They are all written in assembly language. Input to the programs is through IBM 3270 or compatible terminals with upper and lower case capability.

The offline programs are also mostly written in assembly language to run under the DOS/VSE operating system, although there are a few COBOL programs. A utility sort/merge program is also needed for the offline part of the system.

All programs require a virtual storage (VS) IBM/370, 30XX, 43XX, or compatible computer; any model from a 370/115 up should be suitable, depending on the load on the system. At Northwestern NOTIS has been run on a 192k-byte 370-135, a 512k-byte 370/138, and is presently running on a one megabyte (1024k-byte) 4331-1.

Printing of bibliographic material with diacritical marks requires the availability of an IBM 1403-N1 or 3203-4 or -5 printer with the ALA library print train.

Disk storage space adequate for the size of the desired online

Kenton Andersen is senior library programmer at the Northwestern University Library.

files must be provided. Additional disk storage is needed for work areas, and two or more nine-track magnetic tapes drives are required for file backup, system maintenance, and work files. All of the files use the SAM and VSAM access methods; no DAM or ISAM files are used.

Technical Service Component

As of December 1980, the online database consisted of bibliographic and holdings records for approximately 425,000 titles, representing all serials, current and retrospective, held by the main and branch libraries of Northwestern, plus almost all books acquired since 1970. In any year, the number of order records in the file varies from 50,000 to 85,000.

The system supports multiple "institutions." At present it is used not only by all the libraries on the Evanston campus of Northwestern, but by the Northwestern Law and Medical Libraries on the Chicago Campus and the Garrett-Evangelical and Seabury Western Theological Seminaries in Evanston. Each library has its own "file" of records, which only it can create and update. To the searcher, the combined files appear as a "union catalog."

Preorder Searching. At the point where an item is requested to be ordered, a search is made of the database. Searching is accomplished by means of a file of precoordinated, brief entry index records. Each index record consists of a "heading" (an author or a title), followed by data which qualifies that heading and distinguishes one work from another. Index records may be approached generically, using a search term which consists of the first few letters or words from a heading. A search term retrieves all entries which begin with the search term and displays them in browsable "pages" of up to sixteen index entries per page. If there are large numbers of matches on a search term, a group of "guide terms" is displayed for use in narrowing the search. If the desired item is identified from the index, the operator may then request a display of bibliographic data, copy/volume/issue level holdings, order information, and/or processing status.

Record Creation. If the search function reveals that the library does not have the requested item, and if it is not on order, the operator creates a bibliographic record, with brief, "provisional" data. Creation of the record causes the author and title indexes to be immediately updated and ensures that a duplicate will not be ordered.

141

Bibliographic data sufficient for ordering is acquired either by direct keying or from the LC/MARC file, which is maintained on tape. Retrieving a record from the LC/MARC database involves a search (performed on a batch basis) of a disk-based index of LC card numbers, ISBNs, ISSNs, and search keys. The operator, after having created the minimal bibliographic record, issues a command code which causes a "search request" record to be created and transferred to a special MARC search file. Each morning the search requests created during the previous day are passed against the LC/MARC index, and if matches are found, the records are retrieved from the MARC tapes. These found records are either transferred directly into the library online file or printed out for review. If a search of the MARC file is unsuccessful, the search request is retained in the search request file for a specified period of time and processed against each weekly subscription tape when it is received.

If no LC/MARC record is available, the operator can enter full bibliographic data (using NUC copy) or can input "provisional" data, sufficient for use in ordering.

At the point of creation of the bibliographic record, the operator also creates a "copy holdings" record, which is linked to the bibliographic record. This record contains local "title level" data (date of creation, cataloging status, search trail, etc.), plus one "copy statement" for each copy of a work held or on order. At the preorder point this statement usually contains just the tentative location of the work, plus a code which identifies it as single colume or multi-volume.

Order Record Creation. Once the bibliographic record and copy holdings records are set up, the operator then creates an order record, which is automatically linked to one or more of the copy statements in the copy holdings record.

Each morning a batch program is run which prints out the purchase orders for the previous day. These orders are two-part, with both parts going to the vendor, who is instructed to return the second part (the report slip) with the shipment. The order contains the vendor's full name and address and is ready for placement in a window envelope. No hard copy of the order is retained by the library, since all information on the order is available online, searchable either by order number or author or title.

Receipt Recording. All items received are checked-in online. This applies regardless of whether the item is a single issue of a periodical or a multi-volume set, whether the item was firm ordered or received on an approval plan or as part of a continuation order. Monographs are checked in by changing the order status code. Issues of serials are checked in by recording the volume and issue number and date in a "receipt statement."

Payment Recording. Payments made against an order are recorded in the order record by means of "pay statements," consisting of data such as the vendor's invoice number and date, the amount of the payment, the fund against which the payment is to be made, and the volumes/issues covered by the payment.

Claiming. Claiming overdue items is accomplished by means of "action dates." The first action date in an order is set to the date by which the first shipment on the order should be received. If the order is for a standing order for a serial or set, as each volume or issue is checked in, a new action date is calculated which is the date by which the next issue should logically be received. Action dates are calculated automatically, but may be overridden by the operator. If the statement containing the action date is not modified by that date, the record number appears in a daily list of expired action dates. The operator displays the record and then decides if a claim is appropriate and the type of claim needed.

Claiming is accomplished by means of a customized correspondence generator. A "memo statement" is created, which contains one or more short mnemonic codes, augmented, if appropriate, by the identification of the volume or issue being claimed. A batch program is run the next morning which produces a window-envelope-ready letter to the vendor, on which each of the codes has been "exploded" into a full text paragraph, and into which the variable volume/issue identification data has been inserted in the proper place. The letter is complete with bibliographic data and vendor name and address.

This correspondence generator can also be used to request that an order be cancelled, to explain the return of defective items, to request that an invoice or credit memo be sent, or to produce a variety of other letters to vendors.

Cataloging and Catalog Maintenance. After the item is checked in to the order record, an operator issues a code which causes a "cataloger worksheet" to be produced. This worksheet accompanies the piece to the search section or the catalog department. In many cases, this worksheet will reflect LC/MARC data, either as a result of a preorder transfer from the LC/MARC file or transfer in during the time the item was on order. Where full copy is available, the cataloger needs only to make a cursory check of the data and assign the final call number. If the initial bibliographic data was incomplete or provisional, the cataloger supplies full cataloging data. After the cataloger is satisfied with the data, an operator calls up the online record, modifies it appropriately, and issues a special function code which results in production of catalog cards. These catalog card requests are accumulated in a journal file, and once a week the catalog cards are printed, presorted according to the library and the type of catalog into which they are to be filed.

The bibliographic and holdings data remain online indefinitely and may be modified to reflect added copies and volumes, transfers and withdrawals, and changes in headings.

Authority control is facilitated since all used headings appear in the index in alphabetic order. To further assist in authority work, an online authority file is maintained. Records in this file are in the MARC authority format, with provision for all cross references, including general explanatory references.

Book Materials. In addition to the printing of catalog cards, the system produces a label for the pocket of the book, a punched inventory card and a punched circulation card. The circulation card goes into the pocket of the book and serves as input to the circulation system. The inventory card is used to update an "inventory file" which is maintained on tape and consists of one record for each volume in the collection. The control number for this inventory record and for the circulation system is the call number itself.

Circulation Component

Books are charged out by inserting the punched circulation card and a punched user identification badge into a terminal consisting of a badge reader, a card reader, a keyboard, and a printer. A printed "date due" slip is produced as evidence of the charge. One of the features of the circulation system is that the user can charge books out on a "self-service" basis.

Discharge is accomplished by selecting the discharge function and feeding the punched circulation card into the reader. If a book is discharged which has been "saved" by another user, a printed message is produced which alerts the operator to place the book on a "save" shelf rather than sending it back to the stacks.

Produced nightly are book-needed notices, book-available notices, and fine notices. These are pre-addressed, ready for window envelopes. A weekly batch program produces overdue notices for students. A quarterly batch program produces reminders to the faculty of books charged to them.

Circulation staff members use CRT terminals to inquire into the file of circulation records and to place "saves" on books wanted by patrons. An online file of library patrons is also maintained.

Patron Access

The most recent refinement of NOTIS is a patron access interface. This interface provides access using the same indexes as used by technical services staff and operates on the same data used for the various library functions. It utilizes a simple user query language and displays data in a format which is maximally intelligible to the user. This interface (termed LUIS, short for Library User Information Service), enables the patron, using any of a number of terminals located in public service areas, to locate books and serials. Once it has been determined that the library has a work, the patron switches to a circulation inquiry screen, which can be used to determine if the book is actually available.

Planned Refinements

The indexes are being redesigned to allow subject access, to provide a greater level of authority control, to supply cross references, and to improve collocation. The bibliographic subsystem is being revised to provide for the automatic linkage of analytic records with their containing items. It is anticipated that these refinements will be operational in early 1981. For the longer term, it is planned to add a call number index and to make improvements to the circulation system.

UNIVERSITY OF CALIFORNIA, LOS ANGELES

The UCLA Library Technical Processing System (TPS) is an outgrowth of the Biomedical Library Technical Processing System developed in 1970. The new system is designed to serve the campus network of twenty libraries, including four major technical processing centers. The TPS is undergoing major software modi-

Written by Dan Tonkery, associate university librarian for technical and bibliographical product services at the University of California — Los Angeles.

145

fications to support the requirements of a MARC-based multi-library system providing online real-time data input and maintenance for acquisitions, serials processing, and a local online catalog.

Operating Environment

The TPS operates on an IBM 3033 computer under MVS. This twelve megabyte machine is operated by the Office of Academic Computing at UCLA. The applications software is written in PL/1, runs under IBM's Time-Sharing Option (TSO), and requires over 500K for online program execution. The current system supports sixty asynchronous terminals including the IBM 3101 and Delta Data 4100 operating at 1200 and 2400 baud in block mode. With over one billion bytes of online storage (IBM 3350), the TPS supports thirty different online data files.

Major System Features

MARC Communications Format. Each record in the Technical Processing System is built on the MARC communications format which has been selected as the standard for each database. To the MARC bibliographic fields are added several fields in the 900 series which contain local processing information.

Master Bibliographic Record Concept. The TPS is designed around a master bibliographic record concept which allows only one campus record per title. In UCLA's multi-library environment, this concept required the development of a four-level record structure with an appropriate security protection system to control access and maintenance authorization. Within the hierarchical record structure, a given title is controlled at the record level, the holding library level, and the copy level. In addition, the security module controls the online maintenance activity permitted in the system. For example, any of the twenty libraries on campus may create a record and add their local processing information to that record. However, once the record is released to the system, only a processing center is authorized to change the bibliographic information. The local information is maintained in the master record by a series of branch codes. Thus, each record contains bibliographic information which cannot be changed except by an authorized center and local processing information which can only be changed by the appropriate local unit.

Online Loading and Indexing of OCLC Archive Tapes. In addition to the system capability of creating new records online, a program has been developed to utilize bibliographic information from the OCLC archive tape. Each week the OCLC records are converted to UCLA's internal processing format and loaded into either the local MARC serials file or the online monographic archive file.

This weekly loading process is completed online with simultaneous indexing of the appropriate fields in the records. Central to the design philosophy is the decision to maintain all of the files in alphabetical main entry filing order. Each record from the OCLC tape is added to its proper place in the alphabetical file, and the appropriate indexes are created and updated dynamically.

Advanced Space Management Techniques. The development of an advanced space management system which overcomes the limitations of the fixed length of a disk track is crucial to the online loading and simultaneous indexing of the records in the online files. At UCLA we have developed a modified VSAM technique which has solved the problem of updating variable length records. When a file is loaded onto a disk, the program leaves some slack space on each track and does not allow a record to be split over two tracks. On every few tracks additional slack space is allocated. The online programs which modify records, facilitate the creation of new records, and perform the weekly "dynamic move" routine for records from OCLC can either find space on the desired track or can move records around within a few tracks until space is obtained to perform the record update or addition as desired. The alphabetical sequence of the files is always maintained.

Boolean Keyword Search Access. Each user of the TPS has immediate online keyword access to all indexed fields in a record and may use full Boolean search logic. Thus the information retrieved is always current. As new records are added from either OCLC archive tape or by users during a terminal session, the program creates the indexes and simultaneously updates the respective dictionary files. In this way, the UCLA Technical Processing System combines sophisticated real-time online retrieval and maintenance in one system.

Current and Proposed Applications

Serials System. The UCLA MARC serials file contains over 35,000 records which are maintained online. In addition to the online serials edit system, approximately 30,000 brief machine-readable records for serials have been loaded online and are presently being updated to the full MARC bibliographic format. Offline products include a monthly microfiche list of UCLA's serial holdings.

After the data collection phase is completed, the serials processing system will control the order, invoicing, check-in, claiming, and binding operations for over 60,000 live serial titles acquired by the UCLA libraries. Part of the funding for software development for the serials editing system came from the U.S. Office of Education (Title II-C grant).

Acquisitions In-Process System. The TPS implementation team is now working on the development of a complete online acquisitions in-process control system for monographs. The system will include ordering and receipt functions, in-process control, automatic claiming, cancellations, binding, and full fiscal control for over 150,000 volumes processed annually by all units on campus. Weekly public service lists will provide multiple access points to this material.

Online Catalog. Future developments of the UCLA Technical Processing System include a local online catalog with an interactive authority control module. UCLA will soon have a monographic database containing over 300,000 machine-readable records which will be maintained in the online edit system.

UNIVERSITY OF DENVER

The Serials Management System has been in use at the University of Denver since 1976. It is a subsystem of a computer-based library management system which also includes acquisitions, fund accounting, and circulation control. Information generated through these subsystems is available directly to users through public access terminals located in key service areas.

The system, designed by Ward Shaw and me, is fully interactive. It runs on Burroughs B6800 hardware, with access through both Data Media 2500 CRT terminals, hardwired through Prentice Line Drivers on a 9600 BAUD asynchronous loop line, and through assorted dial access remote terminals at 300 BAUD. Programs are written in ALGOL.

The serials system manages 15,000 serial and periodical titles,

Written by Patricia B. Culkin, associate director of the University of Denver Library.

5,000 of which are current. The system consists of the following four programs and files:

1. SER/E — executive control program
2. SER/CLEAN — file maintenance program
3. SER — serials data file
4. IND — index file to serials data.

In addition, there are several short programs used for special applications — generating binding, vendor and claim lists, subject bibliographies, fiche copies of the serials file for remote and union list purposes, etc.

The main data file SER contains full bibliographic data for each title, as well as holdings, call number, notes, cross references, internal record number, binding information, vendor, status, accounting information, issues per volume, and time to receive a volume. Each record also contains a description of each issue not yet bound, a status for that issue, and a date of last action. Manipulation of this data through commands in the SER/E program ensures full bibliographic control for all serial holdings, subscription control for current titles, and accurate inventory of all unbound issues.

All data is accessible interactively. Commands in SER/E include:

1. Check — to record receipt or change status of current issues
2. Fix — to access and update any data element (used for changes and additions to existing records and to delete records)
3. Addrec — to add new titles or cross reference
4. Pay — to access and update payment information
5. Bind Charge — to charge issues to and from bindery
6. Exit — to exit the program.

3-2-1 search keys (first three letters of first word in the title, first two letters of second word, first letter of third word) are most commonly used to retrieve records, but record number and full title searches are also possible. The searches are binary, bisecting the alphabetically maintained INDEX file until the target is located, or until the file is exhausted. Most searches require an average of four to five file accesses, and response time is less than two seconds.

The SER data file is maintained in no particular order. It is a character file with a maximum record size of one. Once the character start position of the record is determined from the INDEX file, the SER/E program calculates from information at the beginning of the record the size of the record and where various elements in it are located. Using direct file read and write capability, it then loads exactly that much information from the file into core and writes elements required by the particular command to the terminal screen. A typical search interaction is in figure 1.

This particular file construction was designed to circumvent the problems associated with the complex and irregular nature of serials data. Many attempts at serials automation failed over the question of record format. Programs to add, delete, update, and manipulate records are easy enough if agreement can be reached on what that record should look like. Given the volatility of serials literature, however, that consensus has never been easy to obtain.

Consequently, it was decided to let history be the only arbiter of the form a particular serials record would take and that individual serials records would be constructed according to patterns dictated by their own particular histories. (History is defined for serials as pattern and schedule of receipt, binding schedule, payment records, title changes, see references, etc.) Because histories vary tremendously from title to title, it follows that universally applicable record formats would be difficult to design and manipulate efficiently. The decision to go to a character file and to give the executive program responsibility for casting records into readable displays for interactive purposes allowed us the luxury of letting each record be only as big as it needed to be, and to expand or contract as activity occurs. It has proven very efficient in program operation and in conservation of computer resource.

The SER/EXPER2 program has the following capabilities:

1. Predict receipt
2. Record receipt concisely
3. Update issue status
4. Update payment information
5. Issue binding notices
6. Issue claim notices
7. Allow full editing and update (add, delete, change any data element).

The Check routine is the system workhorse command. In Check, the system requests and searches the target key and displays select elements from the record. The operator typically does

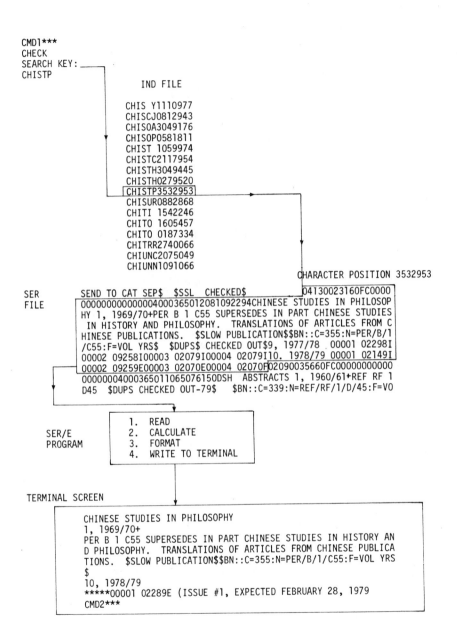

CMD1***
CHECK
SEARCH KEY: _____
CHISTP

IND FILE

CHIS Y1110977
CHISCJ0812943
CHISOA3049176
CHISOP0581811
CHIST 1059974
CHISTC2117954
CHISTH3049445
CHISTH0279520
CHISTP3532953
CHISUR0882868
CHITI 1542246
CHITO 1605457
CHITO 0187334
CHITRR2740066
CHIUNC2075049
CHIUNN1091066

CHARACTER POSITION 3532953

SER
FILE

SEND TO CAT SEP$ $SSL CHECKED$ 04130023160FC0000
00000000000000400036501208109229 4CHINESE STUDIES IN PHILOSOP
HY 1, 1969/70+PER B 1 C55 SUPERSEDES IN PART CHINESE STUDIES
IN HISTORY AND PHILOSOPHY. TRANSLATIONS OF ARTICLES FROM C
HINESE PUBLICATIONS. $SLOW PUBLICATION$$BN::C=355:N=PER/B/1
/C55:F=VOL YRS$ $DUPS$ CHECKED OUT$9, 1977/78 00001 02298I
00002 09258I00003 02079I00004 02079I10. 1978/79 00001 02149I
00002 09259E00003 02070E00004 02070F02090035660FC00000000000
000000040003650110650761500SH ABSTRACTS 1, 1960/61+REF RF 1
D45 $DUPS CHECKED OUT-79$ $BN::C=339:N=REF/RF/1/D/45:F=VO

SER/E
PROGRAM

1.	READ
2.	CALCULATE
3.	FORMAT
4.	WRITE TO TERMINAL

TERMINAL SCREEN

CHINESE STUDIES IN PHILOSOPHY
1, 1969/70+
PER B 1 C55 SUPERSEDES IN PART CHINESE STUDIES IN HISTORY AN
D PHILOSOPHY. TRANSLATIONS OF ARTICLES FROM CHINESE PUBLICA
TIONS. $SLOW PUBLICATION$$BN::C=355:N=PER/B/1/C55:F=VOL YRS
$
10, 1978/79
*****00001 02289E (ISSUE #1, EXPECTED FEBRUARY 28, 1979
CMD2***

Figure 1. Searching in SER

not need to see the whole record, often only the title, call number, and expected issue. (See figure 2.)

If the issue in hand matches the expected issue, the operator need press one key to cause the status to change from "expected" to "in" and for the current date to be supplied automatically. If the issue does not match the display issue, the "all" command and the "previous volume" and "next volume" commands will retrieve and display a complete picture of volumes in progress and any other earlier or later volumes not yet bound. The issue may be checked into these volumes using a line number and a X-MIT line key. A new volume may be created on request. Expectation dates for issues are again a function of their own history; they are calculated directly from the receipt pattern of the previous volume.

The background file maintenance program, SER/CLEAN, run once a day after hours, rebuilds, compacts, and reindexes the SER file to effect quick searches and make most efficient use of disk storage. "Killed" records are deleted, issues descriptions for bound volumes removed (the holdings statement indicates bound holdings; issues descriptions are maintained only for units not yet bound), and new index pointers created for each record in the file. Other background programs, run as required, create target lists of issues for binding and claiming and change issue status and action dates accordingly.

Benefits derived from computer-based serials control include:

```
CMDI***
   CHE
SEARCH KEY:
   CHISTP
0023160
CHINESE STUDIES IN PHILOSOPHY
1, 1969,70+
PER B 1 C55 SUPERSEDES IN PART CHINESE STUDIES IN HISTORY AN
D PHILOSOPHY.  TRANSLATIONS OF ARTICLES FROM CHINESE PUBLICA
TIONS.  $SLOW PUBLICATION$$BN::C+355:N=PER/B/1/C55:F=VOL YRS
$
10,1978/79
*****00002 09259E   (VOLUME 10, ISSUE 2, EXPECTED SEPTEMBER 25, 1979)
CMD2***
```

Figure 2. The Check Feature of SER

1. Reduction of processing time for routine tasks by one half
2. Reduction of staff by six
3. Expanded record access and control capability
4. Expanded public access capability
5. Extension of statistical analysis capability, e.g. payment data, vendor distribution, vendor performance, etc.
6. High interface potential to other systems and services.

UNIVERSITY OF ILLINOIS

The Library Computer System (LCS) now in use in the state of Illinois is an online circulation system which features known-item searching of both monographs and serials. LCS presents a solution to the inventory control and information retrieval problems confronting a large decentralized research library. Access to the LCS database answers the two most important questions posed by circulation and sharing of library materials: (1) Is the item owned by some library in the system? and (2) If so, is it available now?

In an automated serials control system, circulation is often a forgotten element. The difficulties of acquisitions, claiming, receipt, check-in, binding, and fiscal control claim the attention of those developing serials systems. On the other hand, circulation systems are frequently designed to handle monographs, at least initially, and may lack the flexibility needed in system design to adequately deal with circulation control of serials. LCS offers the same level of circulation control for serials and monographs alike and supports the full representation of serial holdings which allows this control.

Development

LCS was developed at the Ohio State University Libraries in Columbus, Ohio, during the late 1960s by the IBM Corporation. OSU first implemented the system in November 1970 and continues to use it as a circulation control system at present. In recent years, the Ohio State version of LCS, there called Library Control

Written by Rebecca T. Lenzini, assistant automated records librarian at the University of Illinois Library.

153

System, has been expanded to include full bibliographic record capabilities, including subject and added entry searching. During the early 1970s, LCS was installed by the University Library at SUNY Albany; the system there has very recently added the full bibliographic record enhancements in operation at Columbus.

The University of Illinois, then, was the third institution to implement the original system, which became fully operational at Urbana in December 1978. The programs were significantly altered to allow a multi-campus approach to LCS, as the Libraries of the Health Sciences at the University of Illinois Medical Center in Chicago, as well as their branch locations Peoria, Rockford, and Urbana, put LCS into effect in February 1979. The University of Illinois Chicago Circle Campus Library began circulating its holdings on LCS in the summer of 1980.

The 1980 academic year has witnessed the installation of LCS at fourteen other colleges and universities in Illinois; the system now supports more than 250 terminals in Illinois and will be expanded to support 400 by 1982. Since Illinois LCS participants are able to search member databases online and also initiate charges from one institution to another online, an efficient network has been established. A listing of participating institutions and a full description of the development of the LCS network in Illinois may be found in Bernard Hurley's "LCS: Automated Resource Sharing in Illinois," *Resource Sharing and Library Networks,* vol. 1, no. 1 (1981).

Description

The host computer for LCS in Illinois is an IBM 370/168 dual processor configuration administered by the University of Illinois and located in Chicago. Programs are written in both assembler and PL/1. A staff of four full-time programmers in Urbana provided the implementation of the existing programs from OSU and created the multi-campus version of LCS now in use in Illinois. This same staff continues to maintain the system as well as plan its future embellishments in cooperation with the libraries.

As presently configured, basic LCS circulation records contain full author or main entry, full call number, full title, date and place of publication, edition, LC card number, and complete holdings information, including location, copy, volume, and loan period for monographic records, and detailed holdings statements for serials. Figure 1 illustrates a basic LCS monographic record.

The serial holdings file in LCS provides online access to serial or

```
Operator enters:  DSC/301.4242B739W

Response:


       1              2
301.4242B739W   BRAXTON, BERNARD              3              4      5
WOMEN, SEX, AND RACE:  A REALISTIC VIEW OF SEXISM AND RACISM$WASH DC 72-91049
      131534       1973       3    ADDED:  780221
 01      001 16-4W STX          0 CHGD    780427/780525 350409081
 02      002 3W    UGX          0 RLOST   780427/780518 350409081
 03      003 16-4W EDX          0 RCALL   780427/780504 350409081

PAGE  1  END

         6        7        8



Operator enters:  DST/131534

Response:
    10   11
301 4242B739W    BRAXTON, BERNARD
WOMEN, SEX, AND RACE:  A REALISTIC VIEW OF SEXISM AND RACISM$WASH DC 72-91049
      131534       1973       3    ADDED:  780221 ————————17
 01     001 16-4W STX          0 CHGD    780427/780428  350409081
9— 02    002 3W    UGX          0 RLOST   780427/780428  348365520
 03     003 16-4W EDX          0 RCALL   780428/780505  350409081
              12   13                    15      16         14

PAGE 1 END
```

1	Call Number	10	Volume #
2	Author	11	Copy #
3	Title	12	Loan period
4	Place of publication	13	Location
5	LC card #	14	Patron #
6	Title #	15	Circulation status
7	Imprint date	16	Date charged/due
8	# of holdings	17	Date record was entered
9	Line #		on data base

Figure 1. Output from a Detailed Search

monographic set holdings. Holdings information may be represented by a single circulatable unit (i.e., vol. 1) or by a summary statement representing several physically separate units (i.e., v. 1-150, describing 150 actual circulatable volumes). The serial holdings field is variable in length and allows for the flexibility necessary to accurately reflect serial holdings. Figure 2 shows the LCS representation of both bibliographic information and holdings for *Time* magazine.

In addition, this flexible serial holdings field may be used to contain notes, marking instructions, check-in particulars, or any other necessary serial information. Urbana currently enters marking, check-in, and acquisition information, as well as bound with or without notes. Figure 3 illustrates the use of LCS to link two bibliographically related titles in the Urbana database, while figure 4 indicates an unusual location as well as bound without information.

Searching

Access to LCS records is provided through dual-level searches. General search keys include author, author/title, and title, as well as a class number search which enables the patron to "browse the shelf," providing one kind of subject search. Detailed searches retrieve and display the full LCS record plus any associated circulation data. These searches include call number, title number (system generated), and line number from a general search. Detailed searches may be limited to the desired copy number, volume, or location, or any combination of these elements. Serials holdings may be further limited when searching; exact year or volume, along with copy and location if desired, may be specified. These serial options help reduce the time necessary to search the system and aid in user satisfaction. Figure 5 illustrates a request for a specific volume, while Figure 6 shows the result of a search limited to the desired year.

Circulation Control

As a circulation system, LCS provides online charging, discharging, renewing, recalling, holding, and snagging for both monographic and serial volumes. As illustrated in Figure 1, volumes which are charged display the date charged and date due alongside the volume itself. LCS also has the ability to distinguish between patron types and assign the appropriate loan periods. In Figure 2, "2W-BU" means simply that faculty members may bor-

```
   1        2           3   4                                    5
 051TIM                TIME$NY        NOLC        42367    5   ADDED:  771120

      6           7
     SER        PER
   01 REX 001   2W-BU   S        CURRENT ISSUES
   02 REX 001   2W-BU            111 NO. 14-26 1978AP-JE
   03 REX 001   2W-BU            111 NO. 1-13 1978JA-MR
   04 STX 001   2W-BU            109 NO. 1-13 1977JA-MR
   05 STX 001   2W-BU            109 NO. 14-26 1977AP-JE
   06 STX 001   2W-BU            108 NO. 1-13 1976JY-S
   07 STX 001   2W-BU            108 NO. 14-26 19760-D
   08 STX 001   2W-BU            107 1976JA-JE
   8   9   10    11   12          13        14
```

1	Call number	8	Line number
2	Author (none here)	9	Holding library
3	Title	10	Copy number
4	Place of publication	11	Loan period
5	Total number of copies	12	Holding type
6	Serial identifier	13	Volume number
7	Periodical identifier	14	Year(s) covered

Figure 2. Sample of Serial Holdings Display from a Simple Detailed Search

```
           DSC/664.105ZE
  664.105ZE      ZEITSCHRIFT FUR DIE ZUCKERINDUSTRIE$BER
  NOLC       853075          1    ADDED: 780169   SER    NENG    PER
  01 SER 001  UNAS         (FOR 28 AND LATER VOLS. INPUT 664.105ZE1)
  02 STX 001  2W-BU         27 1977
  03 STX 001  2W-BU         26 1976
  04 STX 001  2W-BU         25 1975
  05 STX 001  2W-BU         24 1974
  06 STX 001  2W-BU         23 1973
  07 STX 001  2W-BU         22 1972
  08 STX 001  2W-BU         21 1971
  PAGE 1 MORE ON NEXT PAGE.   ENTER PD2DSC/664.105ZE1

  664.105ZE1      ZUCKERINDUSTRIE $ BERLIN   78-646120
       1797870              1    ADDED:  790225   SER   NENG
  01 AGX 001  1W    S        CURRENT ISSUES
  02 STX 001  16-4W          29 1979
  03 STX 001  16-4W          28 1978
  04 SER 001  16-4W        (FOR 27 AND EARLIER VOLS. INPUT 664.105ZE)
  PAGE 1 END
```

Figure 3. Use of LCS to Link Related Titles

Appendix

```
DSC/966.005WE

966.005WE       WEST AFRICA$LOND   19-10194
     1665725                1   ADDED: 781201   SER    PER
01 STX 001 2W-BU S              CURRENT ISSUES IN AFRICANA READING RM, 328 LIBRARY
02 STX 001 2W-BU                1979 JA-JE
03 STX 001 2W-BU                1978 JY-D (BD W/O NO.3182, 3187, 3189, 3198)
04 STX 001 2W-BU                1978 JA-JE
05 STX 001 2W-BU                1977 JA-JE
06 STX 001 2W-BU                1977 JY-D
07 STX 001 2W-BU                1976 JA-JE
08 STX 001 2W-BU                1976 JY-D20 (BD W/O NO.3089, 3091)
PAGE 1 MORE ON NEXT PAGE.  ENTER PD2
```

Figure 4. LCS Notations for Unusual Location and "Bound Without"

```
DSC/05TIM,B=100

051TIM       TIME$NY        NOLC      42367      5      ADDED:  771120
     SER     PER
01 STX 001 2W-BU                  100 1972JY-D
02 STX 002 2W-BU                  100 1972JY-D
03 UGX 004 NOCIR                  100 1972JY-D
PAGE 1 END
```

Figure 5. Limitation of Request to Volume 100

```
DSC/051TIM,Y=1970

05TIM        TIME$NY        NOLC      42367      5      ADDED:  771120
     SER     PER
01 STX 001 2W-BU                   96 1970JY-D
02 STX 001 2W-BU                   95 1970JA-JE
03 STX 002 2W-BU                   96 1970JY-D
04 STX 002 2W-BU                   95 1970JA-JE
05 UGX 004 NOCIR                   96 1970JY-D
06 UGX 004 NOCIR                   95 1970JA-JE
PAGE 1 END
```

Figure 6. Limitation of Request to Year 1970

158

row the serial volume for two weeks while any student will automatically be assigned building use only privileges by LCS.

Notices are produced nightly and include overdues, recalls, lost notices, and purchase alerts. The system can support more than 4 million transactions in a given year with a response time of four seconds or less. In addition, a thorough statistical package produces necessary management information for participating libraries.

Currently at Illinois, serial maintenance is performed in a batch mode with holdings entered online into a file using a designated format and the SUPER-WYLBUR text editor. Information is then batched into the system on a weekly basis. New titles and their holdings are entered into LCS through OCLC tapes via program. Serial holdings are housed in the OCLC 049 field using subfields a through y. Those desiring more detailed information on the 049 formats or any further information on LCS should contact Susan Ulrich Golden, Automated Records Maintenance Coordinator, University of Illinois Library, Urbana, Illinois, 61801.

Serials Automation:
A Selected
and Annotated Bibliography

GARY M. PITKIN

Because this bibliography is intended to complement the theme of this LITA institute, only items dealing with acquisition and inventory control functions are included. This bibliography is provided as a partial continuation to *Serials Automation in the United States: A Bibliographic History* (Metuchen, N.J.: Scarecrow, 1976; 157 pp.). Please consult that text for items published or indexed before 1974.

Allen, Albert H., and Beirne, Eugene F. "On-line Logging In of Periodicals by CODEN Using Interactive Query Report Processor." *Journal of the American Society for Information Science* 27 (July-Aug. 1976): 230-34.

In automating the journal check-in process at the System Communications Division of IBM at Kingston, New York, the authors defined three major objectives: "To make logging in via the terminal at least as fast as other methods of recording; to make output meaningful to the librarian and user; and to keep costs reasonable by sharing with other systems on the computer." These objectives were met through "an experimental computer program called Journal Log In" used with the IBM system called Interactive Query Report Processing (IQRP).

Check-in is online through a "shortened . . . input command" based on CODEN. Each entry included "an abbreviated title or full title up to thirty-one characters, the CODEN, the frequency of publication, the date of issue and the quantity of periodicals received."

Output products include receipt status by publication frequency, receipt status by journal title, list of titles and respective CODENs, and claims list.

Gary M. Pitkin is associate university librarian at Appalachian State University, Boone, N.C.

Aman, Mohammed M. "Computer Applications in Academic Library Operations." *New Dimensions for Academic Library Science.* Edited by E. J. Josey, pp. 86-99. Metuchen, N.J.: Scarecrow, 1975.

The automation of serials control is described as follows:

"Automated serials systems include four main functions: acquisition, fiscal check-in, display, and public service. The acquisition and fiscal functions usually include accounting, subscription renewal, subscription records (historical), and at least some aspects of budget control. The check-in system should achieve at least the following goals: (1) provide efficient, inexpensive, overall control of serials receipts; (2) provide rapid check-in; (3) provide efficient and dependable retrieval of holdings information; and (4) comprise a simple operating procedure.

Current efforts in computerized serials control systems are aimed at producing the following information: lists of currently received materials actually in the library; claim reports for issues that have not been received by a prescribed time; producing of tags for bindery use; orders of new subscription lists; financial records showing categories of expenditures by funds, by subject, by language; and lists of materials not owned by the library that are needed to fill gaps in holdings. Other by-products that can be provided by a serials system are: routing slips for journals circulated among staff members; receipt notices for staff members who are to be notified when new issues of serials that are of special interest to them arrive in the library; lists by branch or departmental library of serials received within some certain period of time; and lists for the circulation desks of volumes at the bindery.

American National Standards Institute. Z39 Committee. *Serial Holdings Statement at the Summary Level.* (ANSI Z39. 42-1980). New York: American National Standards Institute, 1980. 33 pp.

The "Summary Holdings Statement" provides a long awaited standard for holdings descriptions at the summary level. These statements are to be attached to bibliographic records to describe holdings of individual institutions and of union lists. The statement's objective is to define standards "for identification, reporting, and display within data areas at the summary level of information about the bibliographic units of a serial held by a library or other institution."

The data areas are: (1) Serial Identification Data Area; (2) Location Data Area; (3) General Holdings Data Area; and (4) Specific Holdings Data Area.

The "Levels of Detail" are numerically represented: "Level 1 consists of the Serial Identification Data Area and Location Data Area. Level 2 included Level 1 information plus data on the date on which the holdings were reported, completeness of the holdings, acquisition policy, retention policy, and local notes. Level 3 includes Level 2 information (except for the completeness code) plus enumeration and/or chronology information (i.e., volume data and date). For Level 3, enumeration and chronology are reported when both are used on the serial to identify the bibliographic units."

161

Gary M. Pitkin

Axford, H. William, ed. *Proceedings of the LARC Institute on Automated Serials Systems.* May 24-25, 1973, St. Louis, Missouri. Tempe, Arizona: LARC Association, 1973. 128 pp.

The emphasis of this LARC institute is on operational automated serials systems. The focal point is PHILSOM with five papers discussing "Entering a Computerized Serials Network," "The Coordinator's Viewpoint," "A Programmer/Analyst's View," "Maintenance and Design," and "A User Library Viewpoint." Other operational systems presented are the University of California at San Diego's Computer Assisted Serials System and the Regional Medical Library Network's Serline.

The remaining papers discuss the "State of the Art," "The National Serials Data Program," and "Management Problems of the Network Manager."

Brodman, Estelle, and Johnson, Millard F. Jr. "Medical Serials Control Systems by Computer — A State of the Art Review." *Medical Library Association Bulletin* 64 (Jan. 1976): 12-19.

There are four problems that have always existed in terms of applying serials control operations to computer manipulation. "These four problems can be described as follows: (1) The problem of the correlation of an essentially rigid, inflexible machine (the computer) with an essentially uncontrolled (and perhaps uncontrollable) group of materials — serials . . . ; (2) . . . the need to identify uniquely the objects being manipulated by the serials control system — that is, the titles and other bibliographic information — so everyone can end up talking about and accessing the same item . . . ; (3) The need for up-to-dateness in the report of serials . . . ; (4) . . . the general administrative problems of computers such as cost/benefit ratios, the training required for users and manipulators of the computer, and the faith one can have on the dependability of the machine itself."

The present situation is described in terms of "major changes in automated serials systems" and include: (1) the standardization of bibliographic information; (2) the growth of networks of users; and (3) the development of online capabilities, with or without minicomputers. Bibliographic standardization is discussed in terms of the "Paris Principles," MARC, *AACR,* and ISBD(S). Networks are exemplified by PHILSOM and the UCLA Bio-Medical Library's system. Online systems and minicomputers are discussed in terms of distributive computing and questions that must be addressed in examining the utility of a minicomputer.

Brown, June E. "Bindery Records for the Academic Library." *Library Scene* 4 (Dec. 1975/March 1976): 28-29.

With 1,100 current serial subscriptions, Alfred University undertook a study to categorize the subscriptions by subject and to identify per title bindery costs using customized reports from F. W. Faxon Company.

Brudvig, Glenn L. "The Development of a Minicomputer System for the University of Minnesota Biomedical Library." *Proceedings of the Clinic on*

162

Library Applications of Data Processing, University of Illinois, 1974, pp. 170-80. Urbana: University of Illinois, 1974.

Through a National Library of Medicine grant, the University of Minnesota Biomedical Library is developing a data management system operated through a stand-alone minicomputer. The system is to include acquisitions, cataloging, reference, circulation, binding, and serials.

Automated binding is actually binding notification. "The system would produce lists of materials ready for binding for the binding assistant to use for collecting journals from the stacks . . . . If the volume collected for binding was complete, a code would be keyed in on the terminal. The system would then print out binding instruction forms, either upon demand or periodically. The serials holding record would be adjusted to indicate that the particular volume was at the bindery. When the bound volume was returned from the bindery, it would be checked in through the serials check-in procedure . . .

"New journal arrivals would be checked in by the serials assistant by calling for a display of check-in record for the title in hand using a title search key, i.e., the first few letters of the first words in the title.

"The serial check-in record would indicate which issues were predicted to arrive, which issues claimed or ordered, and which volumes were at the bindery . . .

"The check-in procedure would consist of entering an abbreviated code for each issue which matches the predicted issue. If a date or issue number were different than predicted, the record could be corrected on the CRT terminal and the prediction of the next issue would be adjusted automatically. When a journal is checked in, the holdings statement for that title would be automatically updated."

Buckeye, Nancy M. "The OCLC Serials Subsystem: Implementation/Implications at Central Michigan University." *The Serials Librarian* 3 (Fall 1978): 31-42.

Implementation of the OCLC Serials Subsystem at Central Michigan University was designed in four phases. Phase one was to call up the individual title, locate the most complete bibliographic entry, update it according to CMU requirements, and attach the CMU holding symbol. Staffing consisted of "five participants, two were librarians — one with prior cataloging experience — one was a paraprofessional with several years serials searching experience, and two were clerical staff with no bibliographic experience. . . . The project, referred to as Serials Holding Symbol (SHS), was completed slightly ahead of schedule. We searched close to 8,000 records and successfully updated over 80 percent in six-hour days during an eight-week time span."

The second phase "involved transferring the OCLC control number to our manual check-in file still without an OCLC control number . . . . When this verification project was completed, we began to create check-in records and to 'receive' online . . . . Once the terminal operators became skillful at this work, check-in screens were completed at the rate of approximately fifteen an hour."

Identified as "some aspects of the system software that proved problematic" are: (1) "the fact that there are three levels of system use authorization"; (2) "one-word titles or initialisms cannot be searched effectively via a title approach"; (3) "periodicals cataloged under generic title entries are usually difficult to retrieve also"; (4) "a title search can . . . produce summary displays of every record in the OCLC database that matches the search keys"; (5) "only the previous six receipts will be retained on the record"; (6) "weeklies with no volume and number . . . cannot be received automatically by the computer but need the intrusion of the operator"; (7) "some frequencies are not at all provided for in automatic check-in."

Christensen, John O. *A Comparison of Arrival Algorithms for Automated Serial Claiming Operations.* ERIC ED 112 896. 1975. 76 pp.

"Heretofore, methods of claiming issues of serials publications have been ad hoc. The study describes four methods of claiming and analyzes the performance of three of the methods on 16 arrival patterns, selected as workable examples from a random sample of the Kardex files at the University of Utah, that were graphed against a statistically-based claiming algorithm and two algorithms based on the arrival frequency plus a lag factor. The statistically-produced algorithm produced more false claims and usually claimed issues sooner than the algorithm based on the lag factor. The statistically-based algorithm worked best with the medium frequency (monthly, quarterly, etc.) serials and the lag-factor algorithm appeared to work best with the long- and short-frequency (annuals, weekly, etc.) serials."

Clasquin, Frank E. "The Subscription Agency: A Vested Maturity." *The Serials Librarian* 4 (Spring 1980): 301-5.

At the time this article was published, the author was executive vice president of F. W. Faxon, a subscription agency. He states in the abstract that "in this article some of the resources of the modern agency are examined. Specific suggestions for the use of agency information and its value in administration or control functions are defined.

" . . . some of the resources of the modern agency . . . examined" are management information for use in collection development; financial data; subject lists either by LC general class numbers or by local library determination; index/abstract services listing a particular title; inclusion of title page/index as part of a subscription; union listing for libraries in a geographical area; and online check-in including claim notice production."

DeGennaro, Richard. "Wanted: A Minicomputer Serials Control System." *Library Journal* 102 (April 15, 1977): 878-79.

The ability of computer systems to handle serials control is now a reality. Previous attempts, in the early and mid-sixties, failed because "check-in proved to be a far more complex record-keeping problem than the pioneers had bargained for, especially since they insisted on having automatic claiming and other highly sophisticated features."

Even with the current technical ability to develop and maintain serials control systems, "no significant on-going effort . . . with the exception of OCLC . . . to develop an online serials control system" exists. And the OCLC serials control subsystem is active only in terms of check-in.

"It is becoming clear that such essentially local functions as circulation, acquisitions, serials control, and catalog access will be done more efficiently, more reliably, and less espensively on local minicomputer systems which draw standard records from and coordinate with the network databases." The call is for the creation of a "serials control system . . . to operate on a separate minicomputer and sold as a separate system."

Grosch, Audrey N. "Serial Arrival Prediction Coding, a Serial Predictive Model for Use by System Designers." *Information Processing and Management* 12 (1976): no. 2: 141-46.
The purpose of this article is to provide a model for designing a serial arrival prediction system. "The serial predictive model presented here is comprised of two parts: Part 1. Predictive frequency code and library arrival adjustment factor; Part 2. Holdings previously predicted . . . ."

Within Part 1, the predictive frequency code is "determined by past receipt history . . . . If the serial is published on a regularly delayed basis . . . then the Library Arrival Adjustment Factor is employed . . . . The Holdings Previously Predicted are composed of Labels and Values. The Label determines the proper terminology to be applied to the issues identifying numbering scheme . . . . The Values determine the proper increment to be given to the Labels corresponding to volume, issue, part, etc., of a serial."

The second part of the model, holdings previously predicted, "stores the Labels associated with the vested hierarchy of the given numbering scheme used by the serial and the Values denoting the number of subunits required to consider a subunit complete." The components of part 2 "are the Term Pattern Identifier, the Volume Analog, and the Term Levels. The Term Pattern Identifier consists of a two-byte code identifying the string of hierarchical Labels associated with the numbering scheme of the serial . . . . The Volume Analog permits the model to recognize which specific Term Label in the hierarchy is considered the volume for binding . . . . The Term Levels are identified as A, B, C, D, E, F, where A is the highest level term in the hierarchy proceeding through the string until no further levels are needed."

Harp, Vivian, and Heard, Gertrude. "Automated Periodicals System at a Community College Library." *Journal of Library Automation.* 7 (June 1974): 83-96.
The Moraine Valley Community College Library planned an automated periodicals system within the following objectives: "(1) to provide advance notice of subscriptions due for renewal even if a renewal notice were not received; (2) to produce a purchase order, or a replica providing on a single sheet all data needed for renewal; (3) to provide a list of periodical holdings that included the history of all renewals; (4) to claim missing issues of paid

165

and free subscriptions; (5) to produce fiscal and subject area cost reports that would facilitate budget evaluations."

Code sheets were designed for the recording of necessary information for the keypunchers. The objectives were realized and all output products needed were produced.

Jeffress, Iris P. "Data-bind Computerized Binding Slips." *Library Scene* 4 (Dec. 1975/March 1976): 22-24.

The creation of Data-Bind Computerized Binding was developed by Library Binding Company of Waco, Texas, in cooperation with Baylor University. "The system . . . preprints a complete binding slip that contains required library information and bindery data. It maintains a file of all periodicals that are bound and annually updates and prints the bindings slips that will be required during the following twelve (12) months."

Kamens, Harry H. "OCLC's Serials Control Subsystem: A Case Study." *The Serials Librarian* 3 (Fall 1978): 43-45.

The library of Kent State University was one of the test sites for OCLC's Serials Control Subsystem. "Kent State's primary goal in the implementation of this subsystem was to enhance the public service the library could provide for its periodicals and serial holdings." Access to holdings would be provided through an OCLC terminal located in the Reference Department for public use.

"Because of the interrelationship of the "cataloging and serials control subsystems" a library wanting to do check-in must first catalog the title on the terminal, then go into the Serials Control Subsystem and create a Local Data Record for the title. After performing these two functions for each title, the library can then commence to use automatic check-in." This interrelationship is discussed in terms of locating and using the OCLC catalog record and attaching, or creating, the respective local data record.

"Using the Serials Control Subsystem" is discussed in terms of: (1) retrieval time — "the total length of time required to find a specific record in the database"; (2) automatic check-in — "The system has defined only standard frequencies for automatic check-in, and only if a title fits a defined frequency will automatic check-in work every time an issue is received"; (3) special volumes — this is a substantial problem involving how to enter "multiyear indexes and special volumes" and "is caused in part by limitations in the definition field and in part by reason of the fact there is only one each of the current and retrospective holdings fields"; (4) last published issue — "Failure of the system to be able to tell whether the last issue of the weekly publications has been received is a nuisance"; (5) claiming — "The lack of automatic claiming means that at Kent State we had to maintain our manual claiming procedure"; (6) bindery — "As with claiming, the automatic bindery operation has not yet been activated."

166

Kamens, Harry H. "Serials Control and OCLC." In *OCLC: A National Library Network*. Edited by Anne Marie Allison and Ann Allan, pp. 139-54. Short Hills, N.J.: Enslow, 1979.
"This chapter describes the numerous and varied decisions that library administration must make prior to implementing OCLC's Serials Control Subsystem. It covers most of those areas in which they have to make decisions or solve problems during the installation of this subsystem."

The "numerous and varied decisions" are discussed under two headings: "General Decision to Implement" and "Specific Decision Areas." The former states, "The actual decision to implement this subsystem is not going to be an easy one for libraries to make at any time in the near future. They will have to consider five important areas in reaching its decision. First, their institutional commitment to OCLC, including what they expect from OCLC and what they are willing to invest in it. The second consideration involves comparing a library's present serial system with that offered by OCLC both now and with what can be expected from OCLC in the future. The third concerns the amount of work involved, while the fourth area is involved with the related question of staffing to do the actual work. The fifth, and final area, is directly linked to the previous two areas in that it covers the money that will be spent in implementing this particular OCLC subsystem."

The discussion of "Specific Decision Areas" states, "A library desiring to use the Serials Control Subsystem in its entirety must do three separate things with each title in its collection: The title must first be cataloged on the OCLC system, then the library's holdings information must be put into the system, and finally provision must be made for updating this information as a library's holdings change in the future. The first step will be done in the cataloging mode, while the last two will be done in the serials control mode." The remainder of the chapter describes the various problems that must be dealt with during implementation.

Kimber, Richard T. *Automation in Libraries*. 2nd ed. New York: Pergamon, 1974. pp. 97-143.
Automation of serials is discussed under two chapter headings: "Listing and Accounting Systems" and "Serials Accessioning Systems." The former discusses batch systems only and presents a general description of how a batch serials listing is established.

This general description is followed by detailed discussions of each facet involved.

"Serials Accessioning Systems" discusses automated check-in. "The fundamental task of any serials accessioning system, manual or mechanized, is to record the arrival of each serial part in the library. Additional tasks are to place subscriptions, follow-up delayed and missing parts, prepare lists of newly arrived parts and serials holdings for consultation by library users, answer users' queries about the library's holdings, etc." This introductory statement is followed by detailed descriptions of establishing such a computerized system and the potential problems to be encountered.

Gary M. Pitkin

Koenig, Michael E.D. "On-line Serials Collection Analysis." *Journal of the American Society for Information Science* 30 (May 1979): 148-53.

In this time of declining acquisitions budgets and rising material costs, justification for the selection of serials titles is an ongoing and mounting concern. This is especially true as "serials easily comprise 50-70 percent of the acquisitions budget of most academic libraries."

A possible "solution could result from the combination in an online environment of four components: (1) citation data of the sort produced by the Institute for Scientific Information and now available in the *Journal Citation Reports* — that is, not only aggregated citation frequencies, but also journal-to-journal citation frequency . . . ; (2) serials data of the sort contained in a directory, such as *Ulrich's* or in an automated serials record system, such as COPE or ISI's OCS system, specifically, elements such as subscription cost, publisher, frequency, pagination, etc.; (3) journal ranking techniques . . . to assemble utility/cost ratios and to rank journals; (4) systems software . . . to provide the system/user interface — in particular — the capability to enter additional relevant locally generated data."

Three preliminary steps are examined in great detail. These steps are: "(1) determine the particular subject interests and emphasis of the library or information center in question, i.e., construct a library profile; (2) determine a utility/cost ratio for each serial based on the interaction of use and the library's profile, and rank serials in descending order of importance, using citation data as a measure of use by the scholarly community; (3) provide the user with the option of entering additional data pertinent to the particular institution for those journals at the margin, and recalculating utility/cost ratios for those journals and revising their ranks."

The use of such a system is described in detail for acquisitions decisions, binding decisions, and weeding decisions.

Lewis, Gary A. *An Off-Line Serials System: A Practical First Step Into Automation.* ERIC ED 150 980. 1976. 34 pp.

The Radford College Library created its Serials Records System under the following criteria: "an accurate, readable, easily duplicated holdings list was needed; frequent requests for lists of titles dealing with a particular subject indicated that a subject index would greatly increase service; a reliable system for subscription renewal was needed since existing procedures were tedious and caused many inaccuracies; rationalization of the binding process was necessary to give accurate information on materials selected for and actually sent to the bindery; and, as new demand came from management, the ability to produce special reports with a minimum amount of difficulty was essential."

The system is composed of several IBM "card files: (1) Holdings List File; (2) Technical Data File; (3) Vendor File; (4) Subject Cross Reference File."

The first file "contains a record for every serial title held by the library, whether active or inactive. Each record is presented on four different card formats: title card; subject description card; holdings card; and cross reference card. . . . Each record is assigned a unique number called a Record ID."

168

The second file, the Technical Data File, "contains subscription, microform, renewal, and funding data for all active subscriptions. . . . The vendor File contains two cards for each vendor from which a subscription is purchased. The first card contains the vendor's name; the second card has the full mailing address. . . ." The final file, the Subject Cross Reference File, "contains all 'see' and 'see also' references."

The system generates "seven basis listings: (1) Holdings List; (2) Subject Index to Serials; (3) Subscription Listing; (4) Renewal Listing; (5) Vendor Listing; (6) Binding Listing; (7) Record ID Index."

System maintenance is handled on cards through a keypunch located in the library. Implementation history and cost are described.

Martin, Susan K. "Mixed Media for a Serials System: Hardcopy, Microform, and CRT's." *Information Round-Up* (Proceedings of the ASIS Mid-year Conference, Portland, Oregon, 1975). Washington, D.C.: American Society for Information Science, 1975. pp. 111-18.

The University of California at Berkeley has been creating since 1970 a database containing "the basic bibliographic and payment data of all serials titles . . . the conversion has included periodicals, newspapers, monographic series, annuals, regular and irregular serials, and some works-in-parts . . ." and "is in a MARC-like format. . . ."

Products generated are a keyword index, printed lists, and microfiche indexes. The former provides "access by key words to all titles in the data base." Printed lists include a title listing for "each branch and public service point"; a "monthly . . . list of all purchased titles, arranged by vendor and alphabetically by main entry within vendor"; "lists of titles within fund, giving payment histories"; "management reports which indicate the progress of each fund during the current fiscal year"; and "special lists by call number, by branch library, by language, etc. . . . alphabetic and order number indexes to" the "larger . . . payment printout" are now produced in microfiche.

"In an effort to obviate the manual coding followed by keypunching which was necessary to update the file, the library obtained a Datapoint 2200 minicomputer in summer 1974. It is being used as an input and edit device for invoice information; the cassettes are copied onto the Datapoint's large tape drive, which then interfaces with the host IBM 360/65 computer."

This description is followed by discussions on equipment, computer, and budgetary implications.

Morton, Donald J. "Use of a Subscription Agent's Computer Facilities in Creating and Maintaining a Library's Subscription Profile." *Library Resources and Technical Services* 22 (Fall 1978): 386-89.

The University of Massachusetts Medical School Library had a subscription list of approximately 2,000 titles and was under pressure to examine the utility of that collection. "Administrators were prone to note during infrequent library visits that most titles appeared to be read rarely, if at all, and to suggest that many might profitably be eliminated."

169

Consequently, the library undertook a project to identify "library subscription needs . . . in order first to determine which titles should be received and then to use this information to solicit support for appropriate funding."

The computer facilities of the Library's subscription agent, the F. W. Faxon Company, were used to develop "a serials profile reflecting school needs. . . ." The first step was to identify disciplines, or subject descriptors. "First, Faxon supplied listings of the titles indexed in *Cumulative Index to Nursing Literature, Hospital Literature Index,* and *Index Medicus. . . .* Next, Faxon prepared a printout of the library's subscription list after first programming its computer to exclude all titles included in the three indexes."

Both lists were "sent to all faculty members for their identification of important journals. . . . The several lists, coded in each case by discipline, were sent to Faxon, which produced a list of those current subscriptions that had not been selected by any discipline."

Results "revealed that there were 557 current subscriptions costing about $27,000 that could be cancelled and 313 additional titles costing about $22,000 that should be obtained. . . ."

Olson, Nancy B., ed. *Mankato State College Media System* (Computerized Serials Systems Series, vol. 1, issue 5). Tempe, Arizona: LARC Association, 1974. 111 pp.

This document is an in-depth description of the creation of a serials system. The description is divided into three sections: "Data Collection Procedures," "Temporary Serials System," and "Appendix."

The first section includes descriptions, in chart format and card and code sheet reproductions, of coding characters, card types, filling out various worksheets, holding codes, holdings statements, including special types, various notes, update procedures, instructions for catalogers, and procedures for data collection from Kardex files.

The second section, "Program and System Documentation for the Temporary Serials System," defines "the temporary serials system" as "an interim system designed to maintain control of the current system that is now card oriented, to convert it to a tape oriented system and to allow for updating and selected printing of the files that are included in it." The system, respective programs, and procedures are described.

The appendix includes examples of the serials worksheet, coding sheet, green slip, interim check-in card, serials change form, serials up-date cards, and system reports.

Palmer, Richard P. *Case Studies in Library Computer Systems.* New York: Bowker, 1973. pp. 62-67, 74-113.

The pages cited describe automated serials systems at Swarthmore College, San Francisco Public Library, Lincoln Laboratory of the Massachusetts Institute of Technology, Baker Library of the Harvard Graduate School of Business Administration, Arthur D. Little, Inc., and Tufts University. Each description is organized under the following headings: environment, objectives, the computer, the system, costs, observations. In each case the "objectives" section describes the necessity and motivation for the automated system. The remainder of each description describes how the objectives were met.

The objectives of each system are as follows:

Swarthmore College: "(1) Although complete bibliographical information on periodicals was available in the library's public catalog, there was no complete and up-to-date list of periodicals subscribed to by the library other than the periodical check-in file, a visible card file maintained in the serials section of the catalog department. (2) The single, typewritten, occasionally revised, list of currently received periodicals that was available was unable to meet the needs of all patrons of the three science libraries — Du Pont Science, Martin Biology, and the Observatory Library — because of the libraries' separate campus locations. (3) Many of the periodical subscriptions were probably no longer needed or wanted as a result of faculty and curricular changes over the years; they are being continued either because academic departments were unaware of the costs involved or because no simple procedure had been established for terminating them."

San Francisco Public Library: "(1) to produce book catalogs of the complete periodical holdings of the library; (2) to automate the check-in process; and (3) to automate the binding procedures."

Lincoln Laboratory, M.I.T. computerized government documents system: "(1) to provide scientists and engineers in a large research laboratory with improved access to documents and technical reports necessary to their work; (2) to provide laboratory personnel with a useful circulation system; (3) to provide the library with control of classified documents; and (4) to reduce manual operations and speed up processing."

Baker Library of the Harvard Graduate School of Business Administration: "(1) to explore the potentialities of the computer as a tool in library operations; (2) to make serial publications more easily accessible to faculty, staff, and students; (3) to save staff costs by utilizing a computer and other equipment; (4) to write a final report to include all details and technical descriptions of the system."

Arthur D. Little, Inc.: "The primary objective in developing a computerized periodical routing system was to reduce the time, tedium, difficulty, and cost of routing periodicals. . . ."

Tufts University: "an automated list of serials holdings . . . held by the libraries. . . ."

Pan, Elizabeth. *New York State Library Automated Serials Control System.* Albany, N.Y.: State Education Department, 1974. 116 pp.

In designing an automated serials control system, the New York State Library defined four objectives: "to provide a tight control over the claims, subscription renewals, and binding of actively received serials; to provide the readers service staff with significant current information, no more than 1 week old, on serials holdings in the State Library; to provide for statewide use new printed reference tools to expedite research; and to provide a basis for the publication of a statewide union list of serials."

Following the objective statement and other background information are three sections that describe how the system operates, how it is designed, and how it was created. The first section, "System Description: Man/Machine Procedures," describes how the system handles bibliographic control, check-in, claiming, binding and holdings updates, invoice control, subscription renewal, and management statistics.

The next section, "System Design and Rationale," describes design support for control and sequencing of titles, record conversion, check-in, claiming, and holdings statement production.

The third section, "Creation of the Database," describes data elements involved with conversion and how they were determined, the format of the file, comparability with MARC, and problems associated with conversion.

Additional sections describe costs and conclusions. Detailed appendixes provide examples of conversion forms, output products, flow charts, data elements, and computer-output microfilm.

Pitkin, Gary M. *Serials Automation at Kearney State College.* ERIC ED 116 683. 1975. 18 pp.

The first step in establishing an automated serials system at Kearney State College was complete revision and updating of the manual files. Several functions were automated. One was the indication of where titles are indexed/abstracted. In coding, following the title, numerical codes indicating up to five services were listed. Print-outs of holdings then indicated where each title was indexed/abstracted. Also produced were title lists by index/abstract service for evaluation of duplication of coverage.

Another code was established for vendors and was used to verify subscription lists and to process renewal notices.

"One of the most important aspects of serials control that was automated was binding notification. . . . The code assigned to a specific title was dictated by historical check-in data, i.e., when the last issue per volume usually arrived, the number of times during the calendar year the title had been bound, and frequency of publication. Now, the computer produces a monthly list of items ready for binding."

Also generated are subject lists. "A code was devised to numerically represent each subject," or academic department. "The result is computer generated subject lists providing complete bibliographic and holdings information per title. . . . They are now printed quarterly and sent directly to the academic departments. . . ." Also provided for each title were "format of holdings and holdings location. . . ."

Regan, Murial, and Zimmerman, H. Neil. *Computerized Periodical Systems in Two Small Special Libraries.* ERIC ED 165 730. 1978. 38 pp.

This paper is in two parts. The first is "Computerization of Periodical Routing in the Population Council Library" by H. Neil Zimmerman. The second is "Computerization of Periodical Records in the Rockefeller Foundation Library" by Muriel Regan.

The first part describes the creation of an automated system "routing... 150 currently received periodicals to a professional staff of around 50." This was a massive manual chore as "routing slips were prepared by hand" and annual "listings were made, again by hand. ..." Also, there were three different types of routing slips.

Initially, the automated system provided: (1) all three types of routing slips; (2) a listing of the journals available for circulation; (3) a listing of the staff; and (4) a basic listing of each journal together with the names of each type of slip.

"As we went along we added programs to: (1) give a listing of the journals routed to a particular staff member ... ; (2) put a vacationing staff member 'in limbo'. .. ; (3) get a listing of the last 10 journals entered into the computer. ... Later we added a separate data bank for all our periodical holdings, whether they were currently received or not. This listing tells: (1) name of journal and code; (2) source (paid, free, exchange, etc.); (3) holdings; (4) if currently received; (5) if in 'routing' system."

The second part describes serials automation at the Rockefeller Foundation Library. "... the input procedure was to assign code numbers to all our periodical titles, five digit numbers gapped by ten, and to draw up frequency codes, subject codes..., language codes, and special feature codes." This information was then transferred to coding sheets.

"Update transmittals are submitted once a month, around the 15th, and by the end of the month we receive an updated alphabetical and subject printout." These include complete holdings statements.

"Routing slips will be received at the beginning of each month, five for a weekly, three for a bi-weekly, two for a semi-monthly, and one for periodicals of other frequencies. Dailies will continue to route manually."

Runkle, Martin. "Automated Serials Control Systems: The State of the Art." Master's Thesis, University of Chicago, 1973. 92 pp.

The abstract of this thesis states that "the purpose of this paper is to describe and evaluate the developments in the use of electronic data processing equipment for serials control in libraries — acquiring, maintaining and providing access to serial materials — as reported in the published literature." To this end, the author begins by describing the "Characteristics of Serial Materials," which are: "First, proportionally more serial titles are associated with corporate bodies than are monographs. ... Second, serials are continuous. ... A third characteristic of serials is the requirement for binding. ... And fourth, unlike the discrete unity called a monograph, a serial can change."

This is followed by a set of definitions, including serial, periodical, series, publisher's series, set, continuation, issue identification pattern, frequency of publication, issue publication date, arrival date, and holdings.

The next section, "Processing of Serials — The Traditional Library Functions," explains "the requirements imposed by serials on the traditional library processing functions of selection, acquisition, cataloging, binding, and circulation."

The next two sections deal specifically with files. The first, "Bibliographic Files and Access to Records," compares manual and machine-readable files. The second, "Files of Serial Records," describes the serials record as "the authority for titles held and for detailed description of holdings.... There are two common types of card files used for the serials record — the vertical and the visible." These are compared against each other and against the computerized records.

The section on "Serials Control Systems" describes how computerized systems can be used for check-in, claiming, binding, and other functions. Costs are also discussed, and ongoing systems are used as examples.

Sabowitz, Norman. "Computer Assistance in Arranging Serials." *Canadian Library Journal* 36 (Aug. 1979): 211-13.

The library of the Bedford Institute of Oceanography was faced with having to merge two serials collections. "To generalize a bit, we are concerned with at least one of the following four classes of tasks: merging two or more ordered collections; spreading an ordered collection when it has outgrown the space previously assigned it; rearranging an ordered collection (as in converting a subject arrangement to a title arrangement); moving to a wholly new location while executing any combination of the foregoing."

There are only two methods for attacking these problems: "handle titles in the sequence in which they are to be arranged, or, predetermine where each title is to reside, then handle the titles in random sequence.... The second strategy has obvious advantages: in a random move, any number of titles can be handled simultaneously; shelving errors made during the move are not cumulative; boxes can be transported as soon as they are packed...." A computer-assisted method was devised to make the "second strategy" work, and it is fully described.

Salmon, Stephen R. *Library Automation Systems.* New York: Marcel Dekker, 1975. pp. 147-79.

Pages 147-97 of *Library Automation Systems* comprise chapter 7, "Serials Systems." Following a brief statement on the nature and complexity of handling serials, the author describes various kinds of serials systems. "The simplest type of serials system is the straight listing of information regarding each title. The information is keypunched and then printed out by title, by subject, by library (if more than one library's holdings are included), or in any other arrangement provided for by the design of the system.... Systems which go beyond this function and attempt to automate other clerical procedures involved with the handling of serials usually start with the receiving or check-in procedure.... Claiming, binding, and routing may be handled as part of the receiving and accessioning system...."

The handling of these serials control functions in an automated environment are discussed in terms of possible approaches or systems. These are: unit record systems, offline computer listings, offline computerized serials systems, online systems, MEDLARS, and the National Serials Data Program and CONSER.

174

Schuetz, Elizabeth J., and Drummond, William I. *Shelflists and Printouts, an Experiment with Computerized Records; or the Traditional vs. "Well, I'm Not Sure about That."* LARC report 7, no. 4. Tempe, Arizona: LARC Association, 1974. 20 pp.

"This account gives the background and a brief description of today's Periodical Printout for the Pickler Memorial Library of Northeast Missouri State University, Kirksville, Missouri."

The project had as its objectives: "(1) to provide a public record of the periodicals of Pickler Memorial Library; (2) to prove the capabilities of the then new-to-the-campus computer; (3) to answer questions springing from curiosity; (4) to experiment with ways to expand service to the public without expanding the library staff per se."

In meeting these objectives, "the following kinds of information were decided upon as necessary to the computerized files: (1) title; (2) beginning publication date; (3) ending publication date; (4) start month (beginning of volume); (5) source; (6) renewal month; (7) whether bound or not; (8) whether a current subscription or a 'dead' title, for whatever reason; (9) cost of binding; (10) cost of subscription; (11) country of origin; (12) language; (13) qualifier; (14) classification; (15) primary index; (16) primary abstract; (17) holdings."

An appendix contains copies of code sheets and printout pages and forms.

Silberstein, Stephen M. "Computerized Serial Processing System at the University of California, Berkeley." *Journal of Library Automation* 8 (Dec. 1975): 299-311.

The University of California at Berkeley needed "a mechanism which could be used to gain some control over expenditures for serials . . . and to provide better access for library patrons to the library's large holdings of serials." A program to establish this "mechanism" began in the early 1970s.

"The basic master file in the system contains records structured in formats very close to the MARC communications format, with one record for each copy of each serial in the library. Although the file is a sequential file, the records are actually in random order, chronologically by date of entry into the system. . . . A consequence of sequential file organization is the need to completely sort the records whenever a listing of those records is required."

The master file and the file containing payment information are updated through a "language . . . called BASIC FIX. Its ability to deal with MARC records of any type is recognized. . . ."

Output products used in invoice processing include a monthly "printout . . . that lists all purchased titles and all payments that have been made against those titles"; "warning messages for payments that appear to be duplicates, payments for cancelled or inactive items, payments for items that are recorded as gifts and payments whose amounts are larger than a certain threshold volume"; and "monthly notification of invoices that should be claimed. . . ."

Listings for management purposes include "a weekly report for each serial fund, listing all expenditures made from that fund the previous week. . . ."

Also, "the system is capable of producing on-demand listings of all titles in a particular fund, arranged by either entry, call number, or cost, displaying the amounts paid for those titles year by year."

Bibliographic lists produced include the Berkeley Serials Key Word Index and "listings by main entry, call number, type of serial, mode of receipt, library location, order number, vendor, cost, etc."

Simpson, George A. *Microcomputers in Library Automation.* ERIC ED 174 217. 1978. 56 pp.

This document discusses the applicability of microcomputers to internal library operations. The author describes the "control of serials" as "a complex problem for libraries, especially those which subscribe to thousands of titles." Briefly discussed are "the basic functions of a serials control system," CONSER, OCLC, Faxon, minicomputer applications, and microcomputer applications.

Twitchell, Anne, and Sprehn, Mary. *Implementation of the Ohio College Library Center's Proposed Serials Control Subsystem at the University of South Florida Library: Some Preliminary Considerations.* ERIC ED 124 220. 1976. 37 pp.

This document provides the context of a study "undertaken for the purpose of determining, as far as possible, the effect of" OCLC's serials subsystem "should it be adopted, on the operation of the Serials Department at the University of South Florida Library. "

Discussed in depth are: (1) claiming — "A claim cycle will be set by each library for each serial and will specify how many days following the expected receipt date an issue will be claimed"; (2) binding — "The binding component will identify completion of a binding unit from data entered into each serial check-in record by each participating library"; (3) file conversion — "Each library must create a separate machine-readable check-in record for each serial subscription"; (4) check-in record — "The serials check-in record is the online record of holdings and receipt dates but includes other pertinent holding information as well"; (5) creation of the check-in record — "To create the check-in record, the operator enters data into all of the applicable fields"; (6) modification of the check-in record — "Modification of a check-in record may mean an addition, alteration, or deletion of information included in the record, and it may be done at any time"; (7) retrieval of check-in records — "A search key is entered, and the entire OCLC bibliographic record file . . . is searched for all bibliographic records that correspond to the search key — this may include monographs as well as serials"; and (8) check-in procedure — "After the desired check-in record is displayed on the terminal screen the operator will compare the issue received with the predicted issue . . ."

Young, Barbara A. "Computer-Generated Routing Slips." *Special Libraries* 66 (Feb. 1975): 668-73.

The current automated system for producing routing slips serves 310 staff members by routing 180 periodical titles at the Puget Sound Power and Light Company. Staff time is "two man-hours per day. This includes logging in the periodicals, affixing the correct routing slips, and keeping the database current. . . . To facilitate the routing operation, the number of persons on each routing slip is limited. . . . Ten copies of the updated periodical lists are produced each time the routing slips are run and new staff members check off the periodicals they wish to see on these lists. . . . The slips are . . . filed alphabetically . . . to await receipt of the periodicals."

The system is a three-card batch system. The first card is called "card control no. 10" and "contains data about the person and his or her requests." The second card, "card control no. 20" contains the "code number of the periodicals . . . the name of the periodical . . . , the number of copies. . . , the total number of issues of a periodical received in one year. . . ." The third card, "card control no. 30 produces all the exceptions we have found to be necessary to satisfy the special requirements for individual attention to the staff members."

Young, Micki Jo, et al. *Introduction to Minicomputers in Federal Libraries.* ERIC ED 168 588. 1978. 155 pp.

The abstract states that "this book for library administrators and federal library staff covers the application of minicomputers in federal libraries and offers a review of minicomputer technology, hardware, and software. The role of computers in libraries is examined in terms of the history of computers and current evolving technology. An examination of microcomputers as a solution to library problems focuses on hardware and peripherals, including mass storage devices and man/machine interface devices. Systems software is discussed, with emphasis on program development aids, file management programs, operating systems, and applications. Criteria for system selection are identified, and library applications in the areas of acquisitions, cataloging, serials, circulation, interlibrary loans, reference and information services, and administration are explored."

The discussion of minicomputer applications to serials includes establishment and surveillance of policies and procedures; subscription control; establishment and maintenance of bibliographic file control; recording incoming receipts; materials handling and collection control; output generation, dissemination, and reporting; reference and retrieval; and processing nonlocal records.

Index

prepared by Lula H. Pride